FRIENDS'
Provident Institution

No. 1.

Sum Assured, £100.0.0

Annual Premium, £4.8.3

CLASS V

Whereas *Thomas Backhouse of the City of York Nurseryman* is desirous of effecting an Assurance with **The Friends' Provident Institution** for the sum of *One hundred* pounds, an Endowment, for and on account of *Mary Backhouse Daughter of the said Thomas Backhouse* and *Hannah* his wife, of in the County of and hath signed and caused to be delivered into the Office of the said Institution a Declaration in writing, bearing Date the *Twenty fifth* day of the *Tenth* Month, in the Year of our Lord, One Thousand Eight Hundred and *thirty two* declaring that the said *Mary Backhouse* was under the age of *Five years* years, and was related by blood to the said *Thomas Backhouse* in the degree of *Daughter*, and agreeing that that Declaration should be the basis of the Contract between *him* and **The Friends' Provident Institution**; and that if any untrue averment was contained in that Declaration, then all moneys which might have been paid upon account of the Assurance so made by *him* should be forfeited, and the Contract between *him* and the said Institution should be null and void.

And Whereas the said *Thomas Backhouse* hath paid to the said Institution the sum of £4.8.3. as the first *Annual* Premium for the Assurance of the sum of *One hundred* pounds, an Endowment, and hath agreed to pay or cause to be paid to the said Institution, the like *Annual* Premium of £4.8.3 yearly, on the *Twenty fifth* day of the *Tenth* Month, in every year during the continuance of this Policy.

Now therefore this Policy witnesseth, that we, *three* of the Directors of the said Institution, whose names are hereunto subscribed, do hereby agree, that in case the said *Mary Backhouse* shall be alive on the *seventh* day of the *Eleventh* Month, which will be in the Year of our Lord One Thousand Eight Hundred and *forty eight*, the Funds of the said Institution, shall, conformably to the Rules and Regulations thereof, be subject and liable to pay to the said *Mary Backhouse* the sum of *One hundred* pounds of lawful money of Great Britain,

Provided always, that the beforementioned *Annual* Premium of £4.8.3 be paid on the *Twenty fifth* day of the *Tenth* Month, in the Year of our Lord, One Thousand Eight Hundred and *thirty three*, and on the same day of every subsequent year, until the said Year of our Lord One Thousand Eight Hundred and *forty eight* if the said *Mary Backhouse* shall so long live.

Provided also, that in case the said *Thomas Backhouse* shall die previously to the said *seventh* day of the *Eleventh* Month, which will be in the Year of our Lord One Thousand Eight Hundred and *forty eight*, (this Policy being then subsisting,) and no one shall be willing to pay the future *Annual* Premiums, if any, for this Assurance, the Funds of the said Institution shall, conformably to the Rules and Regulations of the said Institution, be subject and liable to pay to the Executor administrator of the said *Thomas Backhouse* or ~~other~~ the guardian or guardians, and on *her* account the total amount of the Premiums which shall have been received by the said Institution in respect of this Assurance, but without any interest on the same.

Provided also, that if any thing averred by the said *Thomas Backhouse* in the Declaration hereinbefore mentioned to have been made by *him* is untrue, this Policy shall be null and void, and all Premiums and other Moneys paid in respect thereof, shall be forfeited to the Institution.

Provided also, that this Policy and the Assurance hereby effected, are and shall be subject and liable to the several Conditions, Rules, and Regulations, hereupon endorsed, and to the other Rules and Regulations of the said Institution, so far as the same are or shall be applicable, in the same manner as if the same respectively were repeated and incorporated in this Policy.

Provided always nevertheless, that the Funds of the said Institution, (subject to prior Claims and Demands,) shall alone be liable to answer and make good all Claims and Demands in respect of this Policy. And that neither the Directors executing this Policy, nor any of them, nor any other Director or other Officer of the said Institution, their respective Executors or Administrators, shall be individually subject or liable to any Action, Suit, Claim, or Demand whatsoever in respect of this Policy, except so far as such Director or other Officer may have made himself answerable or responsible under the Provisions of the Act of 10 Geo. IV. cap. 56; and that no other Member of the said Institution, nor any other person shall be subject or liable to any Action, Suit, Claim, or Demand whatsoever, in respect of this Policy.

In witness whereof, We, *three* of the Directors of the said Institution have hereunto set our Hands this *seventh* day of the *Eleventh* Month, in the Year of our Lord, One Thousand Eight Hundred and *thirty two*.

Examined *Benj.ᵐ Cadrug* Sec.

Entered *B.E.*

John Hustler
Wm. Hoyland
D. A. Smith

Friends for Life

END PAPER
*FPI Policy No 1, held in the archives,
issued 21st November 1832*

A sketch from the original etching of 67/69 Market Street, Bradford, the office of FPI 1832–62

Friends for Life

Friends' Provident Life Office 1832~1982

David Tregoning
&
Hugh Cockerell

HENRY MELLAND · London

First published in Great Britain
by Henry Melland Limited
23 Ridgmount Street, London WC1E 7AH
1982
for Friends' Provident Life Office
Pixham End, Dorking, Surrey RH4 1QA

Designed by Norman Reynolds

ISBN 0 9500730 8 3

Set in 11/13 point Photina Medium
Printed in Great Britain by
Balding & Mansell, London and Wisbech

Contents

Foreword

Edwin W. Phillips MBE
Chairman
Friends' Provident Life Office

When Samuel Tuke and Joseph Rowntree founded Friends'
Provident Institution in 1832 they could never have thought
that 150 years later the number of lives insured would be well
over 500,000, and that the funds under management would
have grown to a value in excess of £1 billion. This is a
remarkable achievement, even allowing for the significant part
that inflation has played in the attainment of the latter figure.

Economic conditions in 1932 were hardly propitious for
centenary celebrations – in fact the intention to declare a special
Centenary Bonus was not fulfilled – but a small pamphlet

entitled *One Hundred Years of the Friends' Provident* written by Arthur Rowntree was published. This has assisted the writing of this history which nevertheless has necessitated a vast amount of arduous and dedicated work by David Tregoning, to whom we owe an enormous debt of gratitude, to be added to our thanks for the important part that he played in the events recorded. I would also like to thank Hugh Cockerell for his contribution.

I hope and expect that this history will be read with interest by many friends of the Office; and not only with interest, but with great pride, by those who serve it now or have done in the past. We owe much to that past, and I am confident that Friends' Provident will continue to flourish, and that posterity will record many further notable achievements.

Introduction

In 1832 THE Friends' Provident was born into a time of social ferment. The industrial revolution of the previous 70 years had turned Britain from an agricultural nation into the leading manufacturer of the world. The application of steam power had done the trick. Already steam engines were in use on the Stockton and Darlington and the Liverpool and Manchester railways. They presaged the dawn of the great industrial age. But meanwhile social and political institutions were proving out of date. The Elizabethan Poor Law, still in force, was ill adapted to cope with the needs of shifting populations, and the poor found difficulty in getting the relief they needed. Civic government was hopelessly inefficient and many of the new manufacturing towns were as yet not incorporated, lacking parliamentary representation whereas scores of ancient boroughs, sometimes depopulated, sent members to Westminster. Reform had been delayed by the reaction that set in after the Napoleonic Wars. Although the Tory Duke of Wellington had in 1830 given way as Prime Minister to the Whig, Earl Grey, the House of Lords continued to reject Grey's Reform Bill. Popular feeling was so high that King William IV cancelled his attendance at the Lord Mayor's Banquet, and the windows of Wellington's house at No 1 Piccadilly were broken by the mob. Even when at last the House of Lords gave way and passed Lord John Russell's Reform Act of 1832 it marked only a small advance towards universal suffrage. The mass of the people, tenants at low rents, remained unenfranchised. Democracy was for many still a dirty word.

The only working-class organisations that Parliament viewed with a benevolent eye were Friendly Societies in which people banded together and paid small regular contributions which went to relieve their needs in the event of sickness or death. There were over 10,000 such societies many of which were, it is suspected, run on unsound lines.

Often they met in public houses and attendance for the purpose of paying subscriptions tended to lead to excessive drinking. Parliament made periodic efforts to regulate their rules and to ensure their financial soundness. A system of statutory control, difficult to enforce, had been instituted. Church of England clergy were among the first to register under the Friendly Societies Act 1829 for the purpose of granting life assurance and annuities, founding the Clergy Mutual Assurance Society.

It was a time when the air was thick with ideas for starting new life assurance societies. Anybody could form such a society and many people did, foreseeing a large custom from the rapidly growing middle classes. In the boom years 1824–26 over 20 societies had been floated, which almost doubled the number of life offices. Some failed rapidly but by 1830 there were 29 life societies in being. The oldest and largest was the Equitable Life of 1762 with nearly 9,000 members and a staff of eight. Its funds approached £9 million but it was on a downward trend as competition intensified. Between 1830 and 1844, 56 offices were successfully established, not counting the notorious Independent West Middlesex (1836–40) which proclaimed a (non-existent) capital of £1 million, and in its short life collected £200,000 as consideration for annuities. That failure was to make a deep impression on the public. Both Dickens in *Martin Chuzzlewit* and Thackeray in *The Great Hoggarty Diamond* wrote of fraudulent life offices.

The pitfalls for life assurance at this time were many. Anyone could style himself an actuary as there was no professional body concerning itself with standards and practice until 1848. In 1829 one well respected and still surviving office found itself short of £39,000 when a banker who was a director and trustee absconded to America with the proceeds of exchequer bills entrusted to the care of his bank which went into liquidation.

Life assurance was often concerned less with the original purpose of the business, which was to enable a man to provide for dependants in the event of his death, than with the provision of security for loans, often granted to improvident persons. Annuities too were commonly effected on a speculative basis. They could be taken out on the lives of persons thought likely to live long who had no connection with the person effecting the contract.

Lives were shorter in the 1830s. Tuberculosis and typhoid took their toll and the unfamiliar disease of cholera had just made its appearance. Its causation was not known. All feared it, though the victims were mainly town slum dwellers. No doubt the continued presence of cholera in York, where 185 people died of it in 1832, lent urgency to the concern of Friends of Ackworth in founding their life office for Quakers. They rightly judged that they could expect favourable terms for better-than-average lives because of their temperate way of living.

Friends had many advantages for their enterprise. The tenets of Quakerism included sensible and strict rules for the conduct of business. The stress was on honesty and proper accounting. The exclusion of Quakers from many occupations because of religious tests had caused them to turn in disproportionate numbers to industry and commerce, and there was no shortage of solid guarantors to see a new venture over its first perilous years. Quakers saw it as part of their duty to serve as directors without remuneration. The system of local, regional and national Meetings ensured personal contact among members, so that news of the Institution could be widely and rapidly spread among prospective policyholders.

Bradford was the first home of the new enterprise, a choice which is at first sight puzzling. Bradford was one of a number of centres with a thriving Quaker community but its location was not as convenient as York or Leeds, and it boasted few environmental attractions. It was an industrial town that had come to be known as Worstedopolis. In 1801 it had one mill. By 1841 the number was 67. Between 1821 and 1831 its population grew by two-thirds. Asa Briggs has called it 'a settlement rather than a community'. It was not to be incorporated until 1847. There was in Bradford an undercurrent of industrial unrest which rose to the surface in many riots in the 1830s and 1840s but these were outside Quaker experience. It was from a Bradford manufacturer that Richard Oastler learned in 1830 of the employment conditions of children in mills which led to the long continued struggle to limit the hours of labour for children and young people to 10 a day for six days a week, exclusive of meal breaks, a measure seen as ruinous by many manufacturers.

Despite these social and political troubles 1832 was a good year in which to start a life assurance enterprise. There had been 17 years of peace since Waterloo and were to be 22 more. The population of the UK had doubled in 30 years. A temporary trade depression was lifting. The British Empire, apart from India, was as yet only in embryo with the Australian colonies still under exploration, the Canadas agitating for political reform, and slavery on the point of being abolished in the West Indies. In a predominantly peaceful world the British Quaker community with its pacific and businesslike approach could look with confidence to its new life assurance institution.

Chapter 1

The Modest Beginning
1832~62

FRIENDS' PROVIDENT INSTITUTION was founded in Yorkshire in 1832 to provide the security of life assurance for members of the Society of Friends, commonly known as Quakers. This religious community, founded in the 17th century, was distinctive in an age of deep and bitter religious differences, for their peaceful way of life and for the simplicity of their mode of speech and dress. Their numbers were small, no more than 17,000 men, women and children in 1830, but amongst them were men who had great influence on reform and social welfare. Professor George Trevelyan in his *Short History of England*, in describing the problems which the changing conditions brought in the 19th century in the health, education and social conditions of the nation gives credit to the Society of Friends for the part they played in giving leadership where it was needed, respected as they were for their high principles and fair dealing. A general note on the Quaker community with details of a few of the Quakers closely associated with Friends' Provident Institution in the 19th century appears in Appendix I.

The Quakers were a strong community in Yorkshire and amongst those who met in 1829 for the annual gathering of past scholars of Ackworth School near Pontefract were two outstanding Yorkshiremen, Samuel Tuke and his friend, Joseph Rowntree, who first brought forward the idea of forming a mutual life assurance association. In the early years of the 19th century many insurance companies had sprung up only to enjoy a short life, but Samuel Tuke was to bring stability to the new institution over the 25 years in which he was associated with it. He was prominent as a leader of the Society of Friends in England, and a City

Ackworth School centre library c 1879. In this room FPI was founded 1831/32 and annual general meetings were held between 1834 and 1886. Photographs – left of the fireplace Samuel Tuke, right Joseph Rowntree, founder directors of FPI

13

Ackworth School, from the river, an early 19th century print

Councillor in York where he was one of the first directors of the Yorkshire Fire & Life Insurance Company. He was also interested in the Savings Bank movement and the Mechanics' Friendly Society. He and Joseph Rowntree were moved by the concern for a master at Ackworth School, Henry Brady, who had died in 1828 aged 30 leaving a wife and family relying on the benevolence of the Quaker Meeting. Their ideas were discussed with interest at Ackworth until, in June 1831, Friends, again assembled at the School for their annual gathering, received with enthusiasm the proposal for establishing a provident institution when 'it was the judgement of the meeting that it is desirable that such an establishment should be formed and that it be recommended to the Friends of Yorkshire to prosecute the undertaking'. A prospectus was drawn up for the establishment of a provident institution and mutual assurance society to be called Friends' Provident Institution. A strong committee was appointed 'for the purpose of preparing a set of rules, and making the needful enquiries for the formation of a table of rates, and

also to print and circulate the prospectus among Friends'. This committee was required to report back in three months' time, and did in fact produce drafts which were approved a month later.

The first prospectus, apart from advocating the merits of mutual life assurance, described the first classes of business to be written which were annuities payable from the age of 55, endowment or whole-life policies, and children's deferred policies to be paid to the child at ages 14, 21 or 25. It proposed that the Institution should be formed under the protection of the Friendly Societies Acts, 'designed to promote good order and security of such societies'. The prospectus countered any argument there might be that a life assurance association could be regarded 'as showing either distrust of providence' or 'as bearing something of the character of a lottery', adding 'it is obvious therefore that the proposed institution bears at once the character of prudence and disinterestedness'. It advocated the value of the Society of Friends having its own life assurance association because the assumed expectation of life in the

The 'fathers' of FPI

ABOVE *Samuel Tuke*

ABOVE RIGHT *Joseph Rowntree*

Quaker community, living under their strict principles, might be expected to be better than that reckoned by other life assurance companies. It recommended that membership should not be restricted to any 'particular district of the Island but should embrace the Society (of Friends) generally'. It ended by specifying that the Institution 'is not a charitable association but it simply enables those who unite in it to help themselves'.

At the end of December 1831 a large meeting of Friends gathered at York for the Quarterly Meeting approved the draft of the first prospectus, and prepared proposals for Friends' Provident Institution, nominating the committee of 20 leading Quakers, who had drawn up the prospectus, to be the first directors of the Institution and appointing Benjamin Ecroyd, a conveyancer of 67/69 Market Street, Bradford, to be the first secretary. He held this appointment for the next 25 years, initially at a salary of £200 per annum, and in the early years he was the only

An extract from the first minute book records the decisions to found FPI and form the original committee to undertake the preliminary work in the autumn of 1831

member of the staff. His room over a confectioner's shop at Bradford, of which the drawing is reminiscent of Beatrix Potter's shop in 'Ginger and Pickles', was the first home of the FPI. The building was subsequently bought from the executors of John Hustler, the first treasurer. He was a member of one of the leading Bradford families in the worsted trade, and took a prominent part in the affairs of the Society of Friends. As treasurer he received no remuneration. The board, initially comprised of the 20 members of the original 'strong committee', came from leading Quaker families mostly in Yorkshire. Amongst them one sees names like Seebohm, Priestman, Rowntree, Cash and West. The lead from the start was given by Samuel Tuke who was a director for the first 24 years until his death in 1856.

In the early months of 1832 the Committee set to work in a very businesslike way to obtain accurate returns from the registers of Friends in various parts of the Kingdom to establish the experience of mortality amongst members of the Society of Friends. The Clerks to the Quarterly Meetings in London and Middlesex, Yorkshire, Lancashire, Essex and Westmorland supplied the details of births, deaths and causes of death from their registers over the period 1811 to 1831. From this mortality experience tables of rates were drawn up by William Newman, actuary of the Yorkshire Fire & Life Insurance Company, who acted as consulting actuary for the first eight years, and was followed by Charles Ansell, FRS, FSA, the actuary of the Atlas Assurance Company. It was not until 1869 that a new table prepared by the Institute of Actuaries was brought into use, when Joseph Dymond became the first resident actuary of FPI.

As the new institution had no capital it was decided to prepare a Guarantee Bond and this document, dated 24th July 1832, shows the names of 45 prominent Quakers who each subscribed sums of between £50 and £1,000 to make up a fund of £10,700 to meet any liabilities which might be incurred in the early years. The subscribers received 5 per cent per annum on their money, and their capital was to be repaid when the Institution had sufficient funds to enable them to abandon this means of inspiring the confidence of new members. As things turned out no call was made and the invested life fund stood at £7,015 at the end of the first year, when the directors were happy to report that there had been no death of a member. The moral was pointed the next year with further platitudes when they recorded the death of one member insured for £1,000.

Further finance was raised for the 'Outfit of the Establishment' by 23 Quakers who subscribed £42 for this purpose, thereby earning for themselves the qualification of honorary members, as did those who had signed the Guarantee Bond, but had not become members of the Institution by taking out policies.

During the early months of 1832 Benjamin Ecroyd as secretary, backed by John Hustler the treasurer and the directors, made preparations for launching the Institution. The Friendly Societies Acts 1819 and 1829, drafted to protect the security of the members, required a Society's funds to be controlled by a treasurer and trustees, and laid down the form of the Rules which had to be approved by a barrister and a magistrate. The premium tables had to be certified by an actuary. Against these obligations Friendly Societies had privileges which included freedom from stamp duty, favourable terms for depositing their funds with the Commissioner for the Reduction of the National Debt (at the rate of 3 per cent per day), and the right to pay the proceeds of a policy to nominees before legacy duty had been paid.

John Hustler and Benjamin Ecroyd were both living in Bradford and the ease of communications with Leeds, York and Hull, where there were strong Quaker Meetings, no doubt led to the decision to establish the Institution in that city. It is reckoned that the total adult male membership of the Society of Friends in the UK was about 7,000 in 1832, of whom a substantial proportion were in the North. The number rose slowly in the 19th century, reaching 17,000 in 1900, since when it grew to 21,000 in 1960. Thereafter the trend has declined.

Through the organisation of the Monthly and Quarterly Meetings of the Society of Friends 1,000 copies of the first prospectus were issued, and part-time agents were appointed who received commission for introducing policyholders. Most parts of the country where Friends were

John Hustler, first treasurer

The Guarantee Bond

We whose names are undersigned, Officers and Honorary Members of the *Friends' Provident Institution*, being desirous of promoting the beneficial Objects of the said Institution as set forth in its Book of Rules, and to inspire confidence in those Persons on whose account the same has been instituted, Do, by this writing under our hands, intended to be deposited and registered in like manner with the Rules of the said Institution pursuant to the provisions of the Act for consolidating and amending the laws relating to Friendly Societies, declare ourselves willing to be answerable to the extent of the Sums placed opposite to and in a line with our respective names, for any deficiency which during our lives respectively may upon an investigation of the professional Actuaries be from time to time found and by them certified to be existing in the funds of the said Institution and we do hereby bind ourselves respectively to make good the same to such extent accordingly. Provided always, and the Condition of our respectively advancing any Sum or Sums of Money in consequence of this engagement shall be that the same shall be considered as due from the said Institution to the persons respectively advancing the same, and shall be repaid to them respectively or their respective Executors Administrators or Assigns, in ratable proportions with Interest for the same after the Rate of five pounds per Centum per Annum, out of any Moneys or property which may be subsequently found to belong to the said Institution over and above what may be declared by two professional Actuaries as sufficient in their opinion to support the Assurances made with the said Institution. Provided also that when it shall appear to the Directors of the said Institution assembled at a Special General Meeting, that the Stock or funds of the said Institution arising from the Contributions of the Assured Members shall have accumulated so as to be more than sufficient to discharge the whole of the Claims made or likely to be made thereon, and so soon as the said Directors shall declare a Dividend of such Surplus or any part thereof in pursuance of the Twenty first Rule of the said Institution, then the Guarantee and Liability hereby entered into shall forthwith cease and be void, any thing herein contained notwithstanding. In Witness whereof we have hereunto set our hands the Twenty first day of the Seventh Month in the Year of our Lord One thousand eight hundred and thirty two.

Name	Residence	Extent of Liability £	Name	Residence	Extent of Liability £	Name	Residence	Extent of Liability £	Name	Residence	Extent of Liability £
John Hustler	Undercliffe, Bradford	1000	Geo. Crosfield	Liverpool	200						
Adrian Gurney	London	1000	John Sanderson	London	200						
Samuel Tuke	York	500	Joseph Sharples	Hitchin	100						
Newman Cash	Leeds	500	Wm. F. Hoyland	Bradford	100						
			S. S. Gurney	Norwich	500						
Saml. Priestman	Kirkstall	100	John Tipping	Liverpool	200						
John Beardsly	Scarbro'	100	Robt Jowitt	Leeds	300						
			Isaac Wilson	Kendal	300						
John Rowntree	Scarbro'	100	Thos. Richardson	London	1000						
Geo. Rough	Eastdale & Doncaster	100	Joseph Rowntree	York	100						
Benj. Seebohm	Bradford	100	John Forster	Highfields, Tottenham	100						
			James Brockbank	Brandon	200						
Joseph Thorp	Halifax	100									
Jos. Priestman	Thornton, Pickering	100									
John Armistead	Bradford	300	John W. Maddocks	Leeds	200						
E. T. Smith	Bradford	100	William Harris	Crosthwaite?	100						
John Priestman	Bradford	100	Wm. Ellis	Mansfield	100						
James Ellis	Bradford	100	Joseph Marsh	London	100						
William Blunt	Manor, Doncaster	100	Thomas Hancock M.D.	Liverpool	100						
			Joseph R. Pim	Liverpool	500						
Thos. Priestman	Hull	555	Saml. Cash	London	100						
William West	Leeds	100	Joseph Hobson	Bradford	100						
John Thorp	Leeds	50									
Thos. Fielden	London	200									
Edmund West	London	100									
Joseph Cash	Coventry	100									
James Foster	Old Broad Street, London	200									
Samuel Fox	Nottingham	300									
William Forster	London	50									

Benjamin Ecroyd, first secretary

living were thoroughly canvassed and it is interesting to read that only 18 months later all agents who had produced no business over a period of six months were to be replaced. Early reactions however were good, and even before the first policies were issued the directors decided to raise the maximum sum assured to £1,000 for a whole-life or endowment policy, and a similar sum for children's deferred policies, which had previously by the Rules been limited to £500 and £250 respectively.

On 'the twenty-first day of the eleventh month' (according to the Quaker practice of dating) in 1832 the first policies were issued. Of these 12 were whole-life policies and the remainder mostly annuities except, significantly, Policy No 1 taken out by Thomas Backhouse, one of the arbitrators, for the benefit of his daughter, Mary, payable at age 21, illustrating that from the very start the Rules allowed an FPI policy to be vested in a minor beneficiary in the event of the grantee's death. In the whole-life policies a paragraph recited the details of the proposer's health revealed by the proposal form requiring him to aver whether he had suffered from various disorders including gout, and affirm:

> 'that he had never had asthma, fits or any disorder which tends to shorten life; that he had not been subject to violent inflammatory attacks nor had at any time suffered spitting of blood; . . . and was at the present time in a state of good health, likely to live, to the best of his belief, as long as the generality of persons of the same age as himself and in the same class of life.'

Joseph Marsh, first secretary of the National Provident

The need for such a declaration is illustrated by the fact that out of the first 100 policies issued (almost all preserved in the archives), 56 were whole-life policies and of these 37 proposers declared that they had had smallpox and 19 had had cowpox. Each proposal was referred to the directors and individually rated. It seems surprising that no proposer had suffered from typhoid although serious epidemics were prevalent in Yorkshire at that time. Another phrase in the early policy wording requires the Institution to pay the sum assured in 'pounds of lawful money of Great Britain'; a sovereign of those days would be worth a lot today.

By the time of the first general meeting of the Institution at Ackworth School on 30th July 1834 it was possible to announce that 541 policies had been written bearing premiums of nearly £8,000 per annum and a surplus had been accumulated of over £16,000, 50 per cent more than the sum put up by the signatories of the Guarantee Bond. Steady progress continued despite the reports of trade depression and a serious typhoid epidemic. The maximum sum assured was raised again from £1,000 to £2,000 in 1833 and this met with a good response.

In London the two most successful agents, William Hargrave and Joseph Marsh, were designated general agents. Both were signatories of the Guarantee Bond, but as men of resource they used their experience in the initial success of FPI to persuade another group of Friends, including William Cash, an uncle of FPI director Newman Cash, and John Thorp, both FPI guarantors, to form an institution which would admit non-Quakers as members. Copying FPI example it was founded as a Friendly Society, and with a similar Guarantee Bond and rules. This institution was launched in London in 1835 as the National Provident Institution. William Hargrave, its first chairman, insured heavily with FPI, only survived one year, but Joseph Marsh, the first secretary, served NPI as chief executive for 30 years. He kept on his FPI agency for Quaker connections and received an annual retainer. When he retired in 1865 his son continued the FPI agency. His grandson, Robert H. Marsh, was a Friends' Provident director 1904–41. This link between the two institutions nurtured mutual assistance in the 19th century and the friendly association has continued as both institutions have grown through maturity to success over nearly 150 years.

No.	Class	If having more Policies see other	Name	On the life of	When Born	Age next Birth day	Amount of assurance or Annuity	Age when annuity is to commence	Annual Prem:	½ yearly Prem:	Quarty Prem:	First Prem: due	Assurance taken effect
1	V		Tho.s Backhouse	his Daughter Mary Backhouse	7.11.1827	5	100		21	4 8 3			25.11.1848	7.11.1848
2	II	{5.VIII 9.VI}	Daniel Fanaud	Himself	29.4.1793	40	10		55			3 4 1	27.4.1848	29.4.1848
3	VIII	{2.II 25.VIII}	Same	Do	Do	40	100		50	8 9 4			27.10.1842	29.4.1843
4	IX		Henry Nicholson	Himself	28.4.1801	32	500		on his death	11 18 4				
5	IX		Joseph Hargrave	Himself	6.12.1791	41	500		Do	14 18 4				
6	IX		David Hanis Smith	Himself	20.6.1802	31	1000		Do	23 6 8				
7	IX		Robert Spence	Himself	10.2.1784	50	500		Do	19 15 10				
8	IX		Same	Do	Do	50	500		Do	19 15 10				
9	IX		John Thwaite	Himself	13.12.1799	33	500		Do	12 3 9				
10	IX		Samuel Hodgson Smyth	Himself	6.1.1808	25	1000		Do	20 11 8				
11	IX		John Hargrave	Himself	4.11.1787	45	1000		Do	33 11 8				
12	IX		Joseph Marsh	Himself	1.5.1790	43	1000		Do	31 11 8				
13	IX		Joseph Clark	Himself	15.10.1799	33	500		Do	12 5 10				
14	II	15.II	John Armitage	Himself	1.6.1783	50	10		65	4 9 4			9.11.1867	1.6.1848
15	II	14.II	Same	his wife Miriam Armitage	25.12.1789	43	20		60	9 4 8			9.11.1849	25.12.1849
16	I		Booth Eddison	Himself	17.3.1808	25	50		50	14 17 11			9.11.1857	17.3.1858
17	I		Lucy Maria Woods	Herself	4.4.1805	28	25		50	9 1 3			9.11.1854	4.4.1855
18	IX		William Hargrave	Himself	14.2.1790	43	500		on his death	15 15 10				
19	IX		Samuel Holmes	Himself	4.9.1804	29	500		Do	11 3 4				
20	II		John Taylor	Himself	13.2.1786	47	10		60			3 4	11.11.1845	13.2.1846
21	I		Mary Ann Bloom	Herself	28.3.1807	26	20		50	6 7			17.11.1856	28.3.1857
22	IX		John Stort Whitlock	Himself	8.3.1792	41	500		on his death	23 17 4				
23	VII		Mary Witherall	Herself	14.11.1816	16	50		30	2 11 9			8.11.1846	14.11.1846
24	IX		Richard Mark Brown	Himself	15.5.1783	50	1000		on his death	39 11 8				
25	VIII	2.II 3.VIII	Daniel Fanaud	Himself	29.4.1793	40	100		60	8 9 4			24.11.1842	29.4.1843
26	IX		Samuel Seeper	Himself	4.12.1801	31	1000		on his death	23 6 8				
27	IX		John Bellis	Himself	22.12.1797	35	500		Do	14 1 5				

Page 1 of the first Life Register 1832-37

After the death of William Hargrave in 1836 and the appointment of Joseph Marsh as Secretary of the NPI the opportunity was taken to revise the agency system and new instructions were issued setting out the revised terms for the agents. Amongst other details in this document was the omission of the requirement for agents to canvass for further sums for the Guarantee Bond or for the fund raised to meet the cost of the 'Outfit of the Establishment'. By this time the funds of the Institution had risen to £64,000 enabling the guarantors' money to be returned to them.

In 1837 consideration was given to declaring a first quinquennial bonus but it was decided to defer this until the end of the 10th year, and when 1842 came round the first consulting actuary, William Newman of the Yorkshire, had been succeeded by Charles Ansell FRS, FIA of the Atlas, who was consulting actuary to the NPI also. His report showed assets of £84,196 on the Class IX Whole-Life series with liabilities of £60,614 leaving a surplus of £23,582 and after carrying forward 20 per cent of this figure the balance was distributed to all policyholders in that class, with the option to take it either as an addition to the sum assured or in the form of a reduction of the annual premium for the next five years. The surplus in the other classes was very small and Charles Ansell was not prepared to support a bonus for the annuities, or for children's deferred or endowment classes. It became clear however that the forecast that Quakers would be above average lives had been proved correct, but as the annuitants seemed to be living beyond expectation the annuity premiums had to be raised.

It was in 1841 that the first death occurred amongst the leading characters of the early days of the FPI. John Hustler, who had been treasurer of the Institution from the start, was succeeded by Thomas Fowler when the great social reformer, Samuel Gurney, a director of FPI 1834–54, declined the invitation to accept the appointment.

1843–62

During the next period of 20 years the FPI made steady progress. The number of policies issued from the foundation in 1832 stood at 2,139 in 1843 and this figure had increased to 5,709 in 1862. The proportion of whole-life policies was consistent at about two-thirds of the total number but despite an increase in the maximum sum assured from £2,000 to £3,000 in 1853 the average sum assured on the whole-life policies declined from £667 to £663 per policy. The majority of the other policies were either children's deferred or immediate annuity contracts. In their annual reports the directors showed satisfaction with the results despite references to trade setbacks in the country, the cholera epidemics, and the 'deplorable war' in the Crimea in 1854.

A network of agents had been set up in the early days and they were kept up to the mark by visitations from the secretary. They were all appointed in association with the Quarterly or Monthly Meetings covering the members of the Society of Friends in 42 areas in England with only one in Scotland at Edinburgh and one in Wales at Neath. There were eight active agents in Ireland, in Dublin and Belfast.

The office of the Institution remained at 67/69 Market Street until 1862 when the old County Court Building at 45 Darley Street was bought, and adapted. After rebuilding on the site in 1876, this remained the head office until the move was made to London in September 1919.

Benjamin Ecroyd, the first secretary and senior executive of the Institution, must have been a man of outstanding ability and personality. This was recognised, not only in Yorkshire, but also in London. He was joined in 1838 by George Bottomley who, although unqualified, attained the title of resident actuary in 1857 working with the consultant actuary. In 1851 Benjamin Seebohm offered the services of his son Frederic 'that he may gain instruction . . . and make himself generally useful'. He proved an apt pupil, his salary being raised from £20 to £40 after 12 months, but in 1855 he resigned to start his career as a banker. Two years later he submitted proposals for a new basis for the FPI valuation. The consulting actuary, Charles Ansell approved the proposal on technical grounds, but no change was made, on account of the extra work and cost involved.

It was a sad year in 1857 which brought the death of both Benjamin Ecroyd and Samuel Tuke; the latter was regarded by his contemporaries as the 'Founder of Friends' Provident'. He had lived to see the institution in an age of uncertainty firmly established in its hold on the confidence of Friends throughout the UK. As late as 1858 a report in the *Post Magazine and Insurance Monitor* gave details of 40 insurance companies wound up in 1857, and of a further 35 companies then appearing in the Chancery Court. The total number of insurance companies operating in the country at that time is noted as being over 300. Most of these would have been general insurance companies but the stability of life assurance companies could certainly not be taken for granted. It was undoubtedly the success of the FPI which inspired the suggestion in 1850 that a Friends' mutual fire society should be formed, 'taking advantage of our moral position', but this proposition did not gain support.

In 1845 FPI received its first certificate of registration under the Companies Act of that year, which required mutual life assurance companies and Friendly Societies to register in the same way as joint stock companies. In the '40s and '50s the institution found itself among the 'Five Societies', FPI, National Provident, Clergy Mutual, Provident Clerks, and Temperance Provident which had all been founded as Friendly Societies and had grown beyond the limits envisaged for local societies in the relevant Acts. Attempts were made by smaller societies to curtail their activities by new legislation in 1840, withdrawing exemption from stamp duty from any society writing policies for more than £200 to any individual. The 'Five Societies' successfully challenged this regulation; but in 1850 another Act prohibited Friendly Societies from allowing the appointment of nominees. Further pressure in 1852 from a large group of their competitors petitioned Parliament either to restrict the 'Five Societies' to issuing policies not exceeding £100, or to deprive them of benefits of all the Friendly Societies Acts. The petition

No. _432_ CERTIFICATE OF FORMAL REGISTRATION

of the _Friends Provident Institution_ ~~Company~~.

Pursuant to the Act 7 & 8 Vict., c. 110.

———

I, FREDERIC ROGERS, ESQUIRE, *Registrar* of Joint Stock Companies, do hereby Certify that the _Friends Provident Institution_ Company is Registered pursuant to the Fifty-eighth Section of the above-mentioned Act.

Given under my Hand, and Sealed with my Seal of Office, this _Eighteenth_ day of _January_ eighteen hundred and forty _five_ .

Fredric Rogers.
Registrar of Joint Stock Companies.

FPI Certificate of Formal Registration 1845 under the Joint Stock Companies Act

failed but the 'Five Societies' combined in promoting the Friendly Societies Discharge Act 1854, under which they ceased to be subject to Friendly Societies legislation enacted after that date. They became in effect mutual life assurance offices, but retained the protection of the earlier Acts under which they had been founded. Under its Rules the FPI funds continued to be controlled by trustees until the institution was incorporated by the Friends' Provident Institution Act 1915. The loss of the privilege of depositing funds with the Commissioner for the Reduction of the National Debt (who incidentally has not yet completed his task!) was more than offset in due course by the freedom to invest in other ways. Benjamin Ecroyd played a leading part in London in the promotion of the 1854 Act, working with Joseph Marsh, secretary of the NPI, and using his close friendship with John Bright, the great statesman and social reformer, to secure support for the Bill in the House of Commons.

Directors in the 19th century

The original board of directors was built up on the 'strong committee' of Yorkshire Friends appointed in 1831 to undertake the formation of FPI. They came mostly from the Bradford and Leeds area but some from York, Hull and Scarborough; and in time other Quaker communities were also represented. For the first 20 years the directors received no fees, contending that it was the practice of Quakers who undertook work for the community to offer their services without charge. In 1846 a general meeting noted that some of the directors were even not drawing their travelling expenses, and they were requested to do so. In 1851 the annual general meeting resolved that the directors should again consider their own remuneration. This they brought forward reluctantly the following year with the suggestion that fees totalling £400 per annum should be paid. This was raised to £500 by the annual general meeting, and the directors decided that £100 should be shared by the four members of the Committee of Management, and the balance of £400 distributed amongst the remaining 24 directors, according to their attendance record. The timing of their meetings was set 'by the Office time-piece, to be checked by the Post Office clock'. (This method of checking the correct time was followed in many provincial cities and towns until the introduction of broadcasting.) Any director who was more than 15 minutes late for a meeting forfeited his fee.

John Priestman, chairman

In the early years there was no single director designated as chairman. The minutes of the board meetings and the annual reports were signed 'Chairman "pro tempore"'. After 1846, however, the appointment of a chairman was made regularly and from then until 1919 the chairmanship was held in turn by James Ellis, John Snowden, David Smith, John Priestman, John Wilson, Edward West, Frederick Priestman, Henry B. Priestman and Alfred Holmes; two of these for more than one term. The Priestman family gave the longest continuous service to the board, followed over a longer broken period by the Seebohms; Benjamin Seebohm, one of the original directors, served continuously from 1832 to 1871. His son Frederic had only a short term on the staff as a clerk but in later generations his grandson Hugh and his great grandson Frederic covered the period 1921 to 1979 and were both chairmen of the Friends' Provident and Century Life Office.

Actuaries in the 19th century

For the first eight years William Newman of the Yorkshire acted as consultant actuary basing his premium rates on the experience of mortality originally supplied in 1832 by the Clerks to the Quarterly

Meetings. It was on his advice that the proposal that a bonus might be paid in 1837 was deferred until the Institution had completed its first 10 years. By that time the appointment as consulting actuary had been taken over by Charles Ansell, FRS, FIA of the Atlas, an oustanding man in his generation who earned the title of 'Father of the Profession of Actuaries' after the Institute of Actuaries was founded in 1848. He too based his premium rates on the original mortality table of the Society of Friends and the further experience elaborated by the work of James Bowden who prepared a table covering the statistics of all Friends, in England and Wales, over the period 1780 to 1837. Charles Ansell carried out the full function of the actuary from 1841 to 1870 on data supplied to him by the secretary, but shortly after the appointment of Joseph Dymond, who succeeded as secretary after Benjamin Ecroyd's death, the directors raised the question as to whether the actuarial work could be done with less expense in the office at Bradford. Joseph Dymond showed himself capable of assuming this responsibility subject to supervision by Charles Ansell, and by his successor at the Atlas, William Tyndall. At the same time he was instructed to appoint 'a young clerk who would be capable of handling the work of the valuation'. He was certainly fortunate in finding for this appointment John Tennant who was to succeed as secretary in 1885, when Joseph Dymond assumed the senior title of manager and actuary which he held until 1889. John Tennant succeeded as secretary and actuary from that year until his death in 1904. These two chief executives directed the affairs of the FPI for a period of nearly 50 years and must both have been men of great ability and character. They were serving a very small denominational institution in Bradford but there is clear evidence that they were struck in the great mould of the 19th-century Quakers. They were not qualified by examination but were both invited on their practical experience, and contribution to the work of the profession, to be Fellows of the Institute of Actuaries. John Tennant also had the distinction of being the third President of the Confederation of Insurance Institutes in 1898/99. This national body received a royal charter in 1912 under the title The Chartered Insurance Institute. Shortly after Joseph Dymond became secretary the Joint Stock Companies Acts 1856 and 1857 introduced new regulations for life companies, including the publication of annual accounts and quinquennial valuations, in connection with which companies were required to declare the rate of interest assumed and earned, and to give details of the mortality tables used. The FPI was able to conform with the requirement of the Act by having certified by Charles Ansell the 'Friends' 1837' mortality tables which continued in use until after the quinquennial valuation in 1902. The resultant low premiums and high bonuses served the Institution well for 65 years.

27

Conduct of the business

From the start, however, the development by FPI agents was very much restricted. The limited number of agents, appointed only in association with the clerks to the Quarterly Meetings and having no branch organisation other than that in London, could only seek proposals from Quakers and their very close relations or partners. Attempts were made over the years to widen the definition of membership but it was not until the new Rules introduced with the Friends' Provident Institution Act 1915 that non-Friends could be freely admitted.

The annual general meetings were held at Ackworth School from 1834–87 (with the exception of 1854) and manuscript notes in the hand of Joseph Dymond show that these proceeded smoothly except when Joseph Rowntree of Leeds criticised the directors. Dymond recorded 'J.R. of L. grumbled' and 'J.R. of L. expostulates' when ruled out of order. He wanted wider representation on the board – 'Bradford men are not the best men'.

The board of directors frequently had to decide such points as the rate of additional premium which should be charged for travelling overseas. As an example of this, in 1851 the extra for residence in the United States was 15s 0d per cent per annum, with a further 10s 0d per cent to cover the sea voyage in either direction. By an earlier decision in 1840 the rate for a journey by steam packet to New York and thence by land to Philadelphia and Baltimore was quoted as 'a sum equal to three-quarters of the ordinary rate of insurance at Lloyd's for goods'. Another problem came up in regard to the Rule which forfeited the policy of any member who engaged in naval or military service. Members were called up for service with the militia in 1854 and again in 1860 (when many regiments antecedent to the Territorial Army were formed) and members also joined Rifle Corps. Counsel's opinion was taken and it was accepted that the policies of these members could not be forfeited under the Rule even though it was felt that these activities were unacceptable under Quaker principles.

In the early days FPI enjoyed the privilege, as a Friendly Society, of depositing surplus funds with the Commissioner for the Reduction of the National Debt, but after 1854 when the 'Five Societies' lost this right FPI investment was confined almost entirely to mortgages or secured loans to both individuals and public authorities, over a wide range. Railway debenture stock came to be included, but not shares. Loans on FPI policies also grew from 5 per cent to 12 per cent of the funds in the 10 year period after they were first permitted by the Rules in 1846. It was as early as 1853 that the Income Tax Act permitted insurance premiums up to one sixth of the total to be deducted from taxable income, and in

Benjamin Seebohm

that year the rate of tax was increased from 6d to 7d in the pound. During the Crimean War, it went up to 1s 4d in the £1 in 1855, but came down again to 5d in 1858. Income Tax Schedule 'D' return forms for 1877/78 display a depressingly obscure standard of official language which has been little changed 100 years later.

The audit of the accounts was carried out every year gratis for the first 60 years by three members of the board of directors, but a firm of professional accountants, Messrs Barber Bros & Wortley of Sheffield, undertook the audit from 1892 until 1919, when the head office was moved from Bradford to London, and Messrs Price Waterhouse & Company, the present auditors, were appointed. Five arbitrators were appointed each year to deal with any possible dispute over the institution's policies. They were Friends but could not be members of FPI in the opinion of Counsel in 1835 because they could not be regarded as disinterested parties if they were policyholders. When the first claim was disputed, even Thomas Backhouse the holder of Policy No 1 had to resign from his appointment as arbitrator.

The whole picture which one gets from the minutes of FPI in mid 19th century is that the Institution was in the hands of directors and officials who displayed the vigour and acumen of leaders of the Industrial Revolution, strengthened by the integrity and public spirit which were nurtured by the high moral standards of the Society of Friends.

Bookmark c 1910

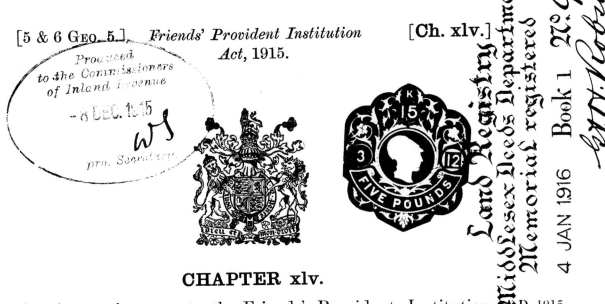

CHAPTER xlv.

An Act to incorporate the Friends' Provident Institution and to provide for the management of its affairs and for other purposes. **[2nd July 1915.]**

WHEREAS the Friends' Provident Institution (hereinafter called "the old Institution") was established in the year one thousand eight hundred and thirty-two under the laws then in force relating to friendly societies with the object of raising by subscription amongst the members thereof a fund for the mutual benefit relief and maintenance of such members their wives children or relations or such other persons as might become entitled under the rules of the old Institution for the time being in force and which might be effected by any of the modes of assurance in such rules mentioned:

And whereas the old Institution is a society not limited by law as to its scope and operation in respect of the amount for which policies of assurance payable at death may be granted and at the passing of the Friendly Societies Discharge Act 1854 the old Institution granted and effected such policies for sums exceeding one thousand pounds and was accordingly one of the societies affected and provided for by that Act and is thereby empowered to make such new rules or alterations in rules as shall not be repugnant to law without being required to submit the same to the Registrar of Friendly Societies:

17 & 18 Vict. c. 56.

And whereas by the Friends' Provident Institution Act 1899 further privileges were conferred upon the old Institution:

62 & 63 Vict. c. lv.

And whereas the old Institution is governed pursuant to section 4 of the Friendly Societies Discharge Act 1854 by rules which have from time to time been altered as therein provided:

Chapter 2

Maturity and Marriage
1863 ~ 1919

As THE COUNTRY moved through a period of prosperity in trade and technical advance FPI developed steadily so that the funds exceeded £1 million in 1870, £2 million in 1889, and £3 million in 1902. The number of new policies written was just under 200 in 1863 and was nearly double that figure by the turn of the century. The business written, of excellent quality, was predominantly whole-life assurance all with-profits; premiums were low and the rate of bonus high. In the quinquennial valuation reports in 1887 and 1892 the actuary described the bonus as being 8s 0d and 8s 5d respectively in the pound of all premiums received. At the next valuation in 1897 the figure was reduced to 7s 0d in the pound due to the substantial fall in interest rates over the period. After the difficult investment conditions caused by the South African War the figure came down to 5s 9d in the pound. By 1867 the actuary had been able to recommend that a bonus should be paid on all classes of business written, including the annuity classes. The chairman claimed that FPI was the first life office to pay a bonus on annuities, recalling that in the early days the better than average mortality profit on the life account had been offset by comparable longevity amongst the annuitants. It was at this time that the maximum sum assured was raised from £3,000 to £7,500, and the practice was started of taking reassurance from other mutual life offices.

The board minutes reflect a number of developments in the insurance industry as it moved forward into the 20th century. In 1870 the Life Assurance Companies Act required offices to adopt a new form of revenue account and balance sheet showing details of their investments

Friends' Provident Institution Act 1915, stamped and recorded 4th January 1916

Joseph Dymond, secretary

and of the claims and expenses. Commission and expenses gradually crept up from 8 per cent in 1870, but were still under 10 per cent in 1904. In 1870 the first Married Women's Property Act came into force, but FPI did not take advantage of it until 1872. In 1894 the first policies were issued to cover estate duty, under which claims could be met before probate was granted. In 1889 FPI became a founder member of the Life Offices' Association, and over the period 1897 to 1904 subscriptions were paid for the work of the Institute and Faculty of Actuaries in the compilation of new tables. The sum collected for this purpose was slightly in excess of the amount required and the Office duly received a refund of £8 4s 8d. It was on these new o^{m3} tables that a complete new range of policies, including non-profit options for the first time, with new rates and surrender values, were prepared in 1903 by John Tennant, almost his last contribution to the work of the Institution, helped by Alfred Moorhouse, who was to succeed him as actuary. The rates were certified by George King, a vice-president of the Institute of Actuaries, who received a fee of 100 guineas. The opportunity was taken to renumber the tables of the Institution's classes of business on a system that has been retained ever since. John Tennant introduced a form of policy rather simpler than that originally used and after consultation with a number of other mutual life offices the scale of extras charged for travel and residence abroad was very much simplified and reduced. In the same way clauses excluding suicide and military service were modified so that claims under these headings could be admitted after the policy had been in force for three years. On the other hand when a member called Dr Friel went as a surgeon with a volunteer travelling hospital (sent out by Lord Iveagh, and not part of the military establishment) during the South African War, his licence excluded death arising directly from military operations.

There were two ways in which FPI did not follow the trend of other mutual life offices at that time. First, Joseph Dymond, after a full investigation of the non-profit rates quoted by other offices, was firm in his decision that the Institution should not offer that type of contract. As he was consulting actuary throughout the whole of the time when John Tennant was the actuary, it was not until Alfred Moorhouse's time that non-profit rates were offered. On the second point, the interim bonus, Joseph Dymond found himself facing a strong body of older members. As early as 1877 he had investigated the desirability of paying interim or intermediary bonuses which were then being extensively offered. The idea was rather cynically supported by the consulting actuary, William Tyndall, of the Atlas, who ended his paper on the subject saying:

> 'The custom has a semblance of liberality which in fact does not exist; and the general public are often influenced by appearances, rather than sound principle, although the latter may on the whole distribute justice with a more even hand.'

45 Darley Street, Bradford, head office 1862–1919

The subject became a matter of controversial discussion both at the board and at the annual general meetings over a number of years and eventually in 1888 a circular was sent to all members, totalling 4,200, setting out the arguments for and against offering intermediary bonuses and inviting their comments. Out of 1,919 replies only 374 were in favour of introducing the new bonus. Even so dissatisfaction amongst some of the older policyholders continued, and in 1898 Sarah Southall aged 97 asked that part of her bonus should be commuted to pay up the balance of her premiums due as she did not expect to be able to enjoy the next bonus expected in 1902. With an annual premium of £55 7s 6d her last bonus was reduced by £96 10s 0d to cover expected premiums valued at £94 11s 0d, and she willingly accepted this offer. Several attempts were made with little success to widen the definition of members but in 1900 it was decided to admit the scholars and teachers at Friends' schools and at other schools managed by Friends, who had attended Friends' meetings. There was little scope for increasing the number of agents, who were still associated with the Quarterly Meetings,

John Tennant, secretary

with no branch organisation, other than that in London under William Gregory, until the position of Cuthbert Ecroyd – grandson of the first secretary – as full-time district manager in Birmingham, was raised in 1905 to that of branch manager. These were the only two branches in existence when FPI took over The Century in 1918.

At the head office in Bradford there was little change over the years but after 1869, possibly influenced by Joseph Rowntree's criticism, at the AGM in 1866, a Committee of Conference, comprised of five leading Quakers, was selected each year to meet the directors and agree the names of those who were to be put forward at the AGM as candidates for election to the board, or as trustees, auditors or arbitrators. All criticism was not immediately stilled as is shown by a letter from an anonymous critic in the *Manchester Friend* of November 15 1872, reproduced in Appendix I (3). The system however contributed greatly to the smooth running of meetings and also brought forward potential candidates for election as directors. The head office seems to have been well run and was able to carry on satisfactorily when the secretary, Joseph Dymond, was given leave of absence to accompany a deputation of Quakers to visit the Australian colonies in 1873, going again to America and Canada in 1874 on ministry work for the Society of Friends in those countries.

There were, however, restrictions, persisting from the time when FPI was subject to the Friendly Societies Acts, which became irksome, particularly limits set on the directors' powers of investment. These difficulties were resolved when the Friends' Provident Institution Act 1899 amended the Rules giving the directors the freedom which they needed in this way, but they were still answerable to the annual general meeting if they appeared to depart from the accepted investment channels or practice. The same Act enabled the Institution to sue or be sued through a public officer. In 1902 the Committee of Conference discussed with the directors the broadening of representation on the board and successfully over the next two years arranged to bring on directors representing Newcastle-upon-Tyne, Liverpool, Manchester and Bristol, and also an additional member from London 'who had banking connections'.

1902–19

The more modern form of reversionary bonus, based on the sum assured, rather than on the premiums paid, had also been adopted for the new series of policies issued after the 1902 valuation when the rate of bonus was £1 10s 0d per cent. A new interim bonus was declared of £1 per cent for the new 1903 series, with a further additional bonus for policy-holders who exceeded their 'expectation of life'. On the other hand, the new premium rates for 1903 based on the 0^{m3} mortality table of the Institute of Actuaries lost for FPI the advantage which the Institution had enjoyed for 70 years by using 'Friends' mortality tables which had produced very favourable terms for both premium rates and bonuses.

William Gregory, secretary

The year 1904 brought to an end an era during which the growing strength of FPI had been guided by Joseph Dymond, FIA, actuary from 1877 to 1889, who retained the appointment of consulting actuary until 1904, three years before his death. His successor, John Tennant, FIA, after 19 years died in office in the same year that Joseph Dymond finally retired. It was a position of strength which was taken over by William Gregory, the manager of London branch who became the new secretary and he was well supported by the very able young actuary Alfred Moorhouse, FIA, who was to have great influence in stimulating the growth of FPI as it moved forward in the changing circumstances of the 20th century. Before his first quinquennial valuation in 1907 he had seen accepted the two major innovations, the interim bonus and non-profit policy, which had not been introduced by his predecessors. These gave the office strength in meeting the terms of competitors.

The Edwardian era saw some modernisation in Bradford office. The telephone, a simple calculating machine and improved typewriters and

*Frederick Priestman,
chairman*

copying machines were introduced. In 1900 Miss Braithwaite had been appointed as the first female shorthand typist. It was however a time of economic and political difficulty. For FPI new business results were poor in 1908 and 1909. A special committee of the board emphasised that inescapably the Quaker community was a field from which only a limited harvest could be expected. In London results were so bad that Henry Harris, 1904–11, was retired and replaced by James Heighton from Bradford. This aroused strong protests from London urging that the head office should be moved from Bradford to London, but this was rejected on the grounds of expense. New agents were appointed and the list of 'eligibles' was stretched to the limit. The possibility of amalgamation with another office was considered in 1912 but rejected by the AGM in that year. In 1914 the board got approval for a proposal to admit non-Friends for non-profit policies only, but the course of world events was to preclude the advantage from this decision.

The Friends' Provident Institution Act 1899 had given normal freedom in investment policy, but market conditions during the South African War and throughout the next decade gave successive causes for anxiety. More than half the Institution's fund was in either well-secured mortgages in the UK or in loans against the Institution's policies, but a substantial sum was invested in Canadian mortgages after the visit of the chairman, Henry B. Priestman, and Alfred Holmes to that country in 1912. A wide range of public authority securities was held and also British and foreign rail stocks, which were reckoned to be unassailably safe, but it was thought necessary to build up an investment reserve of 10 per cent of the total funds of £3.5 million. Nevertheless at his first quinquennial valuation in 1907 Alfred Moorhouse was able to recommend a reversionary bonus at the rate of £1 10s 0d per cent on the new 1903 series, and in 1912 this was increased to £1 12s 0d per cent. The first FPI interim bonuses were £1 0s 0d per cent in 1907 and £1 5s 0d per cent in 1912. No further bonus was to be declared until after World War I, when a reversionary bonus at the rate of £1 10s 0d per cent was declared for the seven years 1913–19. Great changes were to affect the Institution before then.

Miss Braithwaite

The Friends' Provident Institution Act 1915

Early in 1914 a committee of five leading Friends sought a meeting with the board to express their concern for the future policy of FPI and it was agreed to promote a Special Act of Parliament which was to alter the whole status and character of the Institution. The prime purpose of the Act was the incorporation of the Institution as a mutual life assurance office, freed from the remaining restrictions set by the Friendly Societies Acts, and accepting all the provisions of the Companies Act and the Assurance Companies Act 1909. The FPI was the last of the 'Five Societies' to seek in this way the status of a corporate body. It was no longer necessary to appoint trustees to hold property or exercise other legal functions, and arbitrators were not needed for matters which could be dealt with under the Companies Act. As the appointment of directors followed normal company procedure for election it was decided also to do away with the Committee of Conference which, over 45 years, had helped the directors by expressing the views of the members.

J. Thistlethwaite

There were two immediate practical consequences. First, as a corporate body FPI had to have an official seal. The first design submitted by Waterlow & Sons Ltd was described as rather 'paltry' and it was decided to adopt a 'plain and inexpensive seal' until 'a seal of artistic and historic interest' could be approved. In September 1916 the elaborate design incorporating the bust of William Penn surrounded by a great deal of allegorical detail was adopted by FPI, and was later used on the literature of the Office until 1957. The second change was an important personal one. Frederick Priestman, having no current policy, had to retire from the board after 49 years' service (having been chairman from 1885 to 1908) because his office of trustee no longer gave him an

37

ex-officio directorship. Vigorous to the end, his final protest was that 'he did not feel at all incapacitated for the work' – at the age of 80; and he lived on to attain the age of 98.

The act embodied a new set of rules for FPI, the most important change being in the definition of a member. This still primarily required membership of, or association with, the Society of Friends, but the directors were given powers to admit to membership:

'Any person, corporation or company whom, in the opinion of the directors, it is desirable to admit as a member of the Institution having regard to the interests of persons qualified as above mentioned.'

The chairman, Henry B. Priestman, in explaining the purpose of the Bill to the special General Meeting, put rather delicately the new power to admit non-Quakers, including one sentence: 'we are of the opinion that selected lives outside the Society of Friends are about as good as the lives of Friends'. He made it clear that Friends must accept that the directors could not hope to expand FPI further while bound by the restrictions of the original definition of membership, but he explained that the members in General Meeting, either in person or by proxy, would still have the ultimate control of the affairs of the Institution.

TOP *The first 'paltry' seal adopted in 1915*

ABOVE *The 'William Penn' seal, used 1916–57, based on the Great Seal of Pennsylvania, with the motto 'Truth, Love, Peace, Plenty' and allegorical detail*

Henry Tapscott

Thus it was in the unhappy circumstances of the early months of the war that the passing of the Friends' Provident Institution Act 1915 set the stage for the expansion of FPI which had been the urgent concern of the directors and management for 25 years or more. The secretary, William Gregory, nearing retirement after 46 years with the Institution, mainly in the agency field, was not the man to give the leadership required at this most important point in the history of FPI, and no other candidate could be seen either in the Office or in the Quaker community. The board turned to Henry Tapscott, branch manager of the Royal Exchange at Birmingham, a close friend of Cuthbert Ecroyd, the FPI's manager there, who had been involved in 1912–13 in abortive negotiations for the Royal Exchange to take over FPI. He was married to a Friend, Marjorie Brooks, and attended Quaker meetings but never became a member of the Society. He was a strong man of very high principles, a non-drinker, non-smoker and a keen member of the Anti-Slavery and Aborigine Protection Society of which he later served as chairman for many years. He was appointed general manager and secretary in March 1916 and William Gregory retired.

Henry Tapscott brought revitalising energy to head office but in the

Henry B. Priestman,
chairman

paralysing conditions of war the board was reluctant to embark on any expensive campaign of new business production other than urging the agents to take advantage of membership being open to non-Friends. While some of the staff were absent on military or national service, exemption had to be obtained for others, including Henry Tapscott himself who had already volunteered under Lord Derby's scheme. Salaries were made up for those in the forces or serving on other war-time work, and war-time increments were given to those remaining at work. Policies issued since August 1914 excluded death claims directly resulting from military operations outside the UK, and problems arose over claims on behalf of those reported 'missing'. A special scheme offered life cover to members of Friends' Ambulance Units. Investment problems abounded, especially for overseas securities. The block of mortgages in Canada arranged in 1912 carried at $6\frac{1}{2}$ per cent a rate of interest higher than that obtainable in the UK, but when this rate could not be raised to 7 per cent part of this fund was brought back to the UK 'to support national policy'. Property in the UK mortgaged to the office was insured against air raid damage. In 1916–17 however Henry Tapscott concentrated mainly on plans for post-war development. He readily appreciated the narrow bounds within which the agents had had to work, and saw clearly the need for expansion amongst non-Quakers. He also recognised the justice of allowing Friends, together with other total abstainers, to continue enjoyment of the special life rates and bonuses which the experience of FPI had justified, and special premium rates were quoted for them.

As a Royal Exchange man he saw the advantage of seeking life assurance proposals from connections developed in the course of writing a general insurance account. There is indeed in the archives a memorandum signed by him in 1912, four years before his appointment as general manager, when he was involved in investigations into a possible takeover of FPI by the Royal Exchange. In this he proposed that the Institution should broaden its approach to the non-Quaker public by entering the general insurance market before revealing a Royal Exchange bid to FPI members and agents. It was not surprising therefore that when he became chief executive of the office in March 1916 he put forward within a month of his appointment a scheme for opening an FPI general insurance account. Starting from scratch in war-time this would have proved a hazardous venture, but a special committee of the board, with other Quaker industrialists, was set up to study the proposal, which might have proceeded had not Counsel advised at that time that the powers given by the 1915 act restricted the Institution to life, annuity and sickness business only. Undaunted, Henry Tapscott decided to recommend, with the support of the new solicitor John Shera Atkinson, a bold course which was to cause a considerable sensation in the insurance market in the early months of 1918. While FPI could not write general business there was no restriction which prevented investing life funds in the ordinary shares of a general or composite insurance company. No such move had ever been made by a British mutual life insurance company, although the major proprietary companies had gobbled up smaller and less successful competitors over the previous 100 years. The only other example of a mutual life office taking over a general company in this way was that of the Norwich Union Life which acquired from the Phoenix in 1925 the shares of the Norwich Union Fire Insurance Society.

The Century acquired

In the last weeks of 1917 Henry Tapscott approached Henry Brown, the managing director of The Century Insurance Company Ltd of Edinburgh. There had already been speculation in the shares of this company and it soon appeared that there was another competitor in the market, which was to prove to be the Guardian Assurance Company.

Henry Tapscott, first general manager

The story recorded in detail by Henry Tapscott tells how terms provisionally agreed on 12th January 1918 were finally confirmed and accepted on the 28th of that month. It is clear however from The Century correspondence that Henry Brown had not until the latter date broken off his negotiations with the Guardian, and a privileged look at the private minute book of the Guardian showed that their General Court confirmed on 1st February 1918 the terms which they were offering for The Century shares. Their solicitor wrote that day to Henry Brown submitting the draft terms for the contract. The final entry in the Guardian private minute book reads as follows:

'The "negotiations" (crossed out and "transaction" substituted) had been "improperly" (crossed out and "abruptly" substituted) terminated by The Century signifying through Mr. Brown that they had come to terms with another company.'

41

The Guardian were clearly aggrieved by the conduct of Henry Brown, but Henry Tapscott had achieved his objective and it is important to assess what the acquisition of The Century brought to FPI. The small Quaker institution with its head office in a northern provincial city had only two small branch offices in London and Birmingham. The directors, staff and agents were all Quakers and at Bradford, apart from Alfred Moorhouse, there was no one with any great ability. The setting up of a branch organisation to replace the old-fashioned part-time agents, let alone handling the development of a new general insurance account, called for men of quite different calibre.

The FPI agents had made every effort to widen their field by stretching the definition of members amongst those related or associated with Friends in business, or those who had attended Friends' schools, but much of the country, particularly Scotland, Wales and the south east of England, had very little representation. In war-time FPI agents were finding their task even more difficult in areas where the principles of conscientious objectors were not respected.

Alfred Holmes, chairman

In acquiring The Century Henry Tapscott, at a price of £507,500, (15 per cent of the FPI life fund), took over a very well-managed organisation, founded in 1885, its prime object being to write non-cancellable sickness insurance. The Century was writing a volume of life assurance in 1917 almost twice as large as that of FPI, with a profitable general insurance premium income of £348,000, mainly in the UK but with representation in the USA, Canada, South Africa and Australia. It was the branch organisation in the UK which brought to FPI the chance to plan for post-war expansion in fields previously closed to its agents. The Century was well represented in Scotland, at Edinburgh, Glasgow, Aberdeen, Dundee and Dumfries and in England at London, Birmingham, Bristol, Hull, Ipswich, Kendal, Leeds, Liverpool, Manchester, Newcastle, Nottingham, Portsmouth and Sheffield; at Cardiff in Wales and at Dublin and Belfast in Ireland. This was the foundation which Henry Tapscott needed to build up the expansion of the merged offices. In order to simplify administration it was decided that new life business should in the main be written by Friends' Provident, but it was not until the year 1944 that The Century life fund was finally closed. In order to encourage close co-operation by the staff of both Friends' Provident and The Century the name of the office was changed in 1920 to Friends' Provident & Century Life Office, which continued until 1973. In The Century, Henry Tapscott brought to the Office a well-trained staff which gave much needed strength not only in the branches but also to the two head offices which were developed over the next 30 years in London and Edinburgh. Apart from William Robertson, the actuary, and John Little, the secretary, who remained to lead the team in Edinburgh, others like

John Robson, Peter Leishman, Jack Tranter and Jim Swanson brought their skills and leadership to London.

Henry Brown gave up the managing directorship to Henry Tapscott and was appointed chairman. He was nearing retirement age but one cannot help feeling a little envious of his five-year contract at a salary in 1918 of £3,250 per annum, free of tax, with a pension of a like amount for life. As the Guardian had offered him a similar salary it is possibly the pension which secured The Century for FPI. From his personal point of view it is probable Henry Brown expected when he persuaded The Century directors to accept the Friends' Provident offer that, with his appointment as chairman, he could hope to maintain his dominant influence in The Century, of which he had been chief executive from 1889–1918. He expected from Henry Tapscott, aged 41, and the board of a provincial life office at Bradford, a lighter rein than he would have had from an office of the standing of the Guardian in London. It was not long, however, before he realised that The Century board control was going to be with Henry Tapscott and Alfred Moorhouse as executive directors, backed by Alfred Holmes, the influential chairman of Friends' Provident. When the Rules of FPI had been amended in July 1918, to allow two non-Quakers to represent The Century, Henry Brown and David Dreghorn Binnie became the first two non-Quaker directors of Friends' Provident; but soon after the move of the head office to London Henry Brown's thoughts turned to retirement. He had certainly earned his pension, which he enjoyed for 13 years, dying aged 76 in 1932.

In September 1919 the head office of Friends' Provident was moved from Bradford to a newly built office at 42 Kingsway, London WC2, backing on to Lincoln's Inn Fields. This was also designated a head office of The Century and a similar designation, as head office of Friends' Provident in Scotland, was given to 18 Charlotte Square in Edinburgh. The move arranged for Monday, 29th September was upset by a rail strike on that day, but Henry Tapscott was able to organise road transport with one char-à-banc taking most of the staff and important documents, one motor car for senior staff, and a lorry for the safe and other equipment. After a long all-day journey they arrived safely at Kingsway to be met by representatives of the London staff. None of those who made that journey could have dreamt of the changes which were to take place in the next 20 years, but under Henry Tapscott's leadership it was they, with their new Century colleagues, in Edinburgh and the branches, who were to lay the foundations for the development both before and after World War II, bringing Friends' Provident and The Century into the ranks of leading British offices.

The char-à-banc party leaving Bradford for London 29th September 1919

42 Kingsway, first London head office, 1919–28

Chapter 3

The Chosen Partner ~ The Century 1885~1918

THE STORY OF The Century Insurance Company Ltd began with the registration in Edinburgh on 18th April 1885 of the Sickness & Accident Assurance Association Ltd. Its subscribed capital was £12,000 being represented by 12,000 ordinary shares of £5 each having £1 only paid-up. The prospectus, announcing an entirely new form of non-cancellable sickness and accident insurance cover, was reported in both the *Post Magazine* and the *Policy Holder* as an event of special importance for the London market. The company was formed by a group of eminent Scottish professional men, lawyers, including the Dean of Faculty of Advocates, accountants, bankers and leaders in industry, engineering and medicine. The first chairman was James Pringle, Provost of Leith, but he unfortunately died within two years and was succeeded by John Campbell Lorimer who was subsequently Sheriff of Edinburgh. Under his chairmanship, for more than 30 years, the company earned its place amongst the leading Scottish offices in recognition of its stability and good management.

The original prospectus shows that the object of the founders was to meet a demand from professional and commercial men for protection of their incomes which might be curtailed by sickness or accident. Prior to 1885 a number of insurers had introduced schemes for payment of benefit in event of accident, but almost the only form of cover for sickness was provided for the working man for whom no less than 16,000 societies, with a membership of over five million, provided a measure of benefit for wage earners. The Sickness and Accident was certainly the first company to offer a non-cancellable sickness and accident policy in

Henry Brown, general manager of The Century

45

the form which is now called Permanent Health Insurance. The first scheme in this form excluded the first week of sickness but thereafter provided benefit for three months at full salary, followed by six months at half salary, and cover up to age 65, for one third of earnings lost due to sickness or accident. A second scheme of temporary benefit gave immediate limited cover for a period of six months only. Entirely new features of the permanent scheme were that the premium tables were certified by two leading actuaries (from the Scottish Provident and the Scottish Amicable) and the sickness fund, unlike any other at that time, was to be valued each year by a member of the Faculty of Actuaries; John Deuchar was the first consultant actuary appointed by the company. Proposals were strictly underwritten after medical examination and claims admitted only on the advice of the company's medical officer.

A call for this type of policy was expected from the medical profession, quoting the *British Medical Journal*, and from the clergy, chartered accountants and commercial travellers in Scotland. The prospectus also refers to the fact that Prince Bismarck had recently introduced a scheme of sickness assurance for the working classes of Germany, making it compulsory for both masters and workmen to contribute under a scheme somewhat similar to that offered by the Sickness and Accident. As an earnest of the strength of the company's capital structure the original scheme provided for a proportion of the profits, if any, to be paid to policyholders in the form of either cash or a small annuity if they attained age 65.

The first office of the company was at No 1 St Andrew Square, but in 1888 they moved into 24 York Place, and remained there until 18 Charlotte Square was bought in 1904. The first manager was James Black, a nephew of the actuary of the Australian Mutual Provident Society. The *Post Magazine* said that he was 'specially noted for his unflagging energy, a quality of vital importance for the successful organisation of a new undertaking'. There can be no doubt that he tackled with determination his task of setting up a country-wide organisation. The greater part of the minutes of the board of directors is devoted to recording the names of agents and medical officers appointed throughout all parts of the UK other than Ireland. No less than 1,000 agents and 1,100 doctors were appointed in the first year, and a year later the figures had increased to 1,800 and 1,250 respectively. The initial new business was certainly impressive. At the end of 21 months 3,400 proposals had been received, out of which 2,820 had been accepted for a premium income of £7,000, the latter figure being more than doubled 12 months later. By the end of 1887, apart from Edinburgh head office, Scottish branches had been established in Glasgow and Aberdeen. England was well covered by branches in London and the

Sickness Accident & Life Association Policy No 9, 1897

THE SICKNESS ACCIDENT & LIFE

ASSOCIATION Limited.

HEAD OFFICE 24 YORK PLACE

EDINBURGH

LONDON OFFICE 35 Moorgate St. E.C.

POLICY No.
£ 9

This Policy Witnesseth That the Assurance described in the Schedule forming part hereof is hereby granted by the SICKNESS ACCIDENT AND LIFE ASSOCIATION LIMITED, subject to the following provisoes, and to the special provisions (if any) contained in the Schedule :—

(1) That the proposal and declaration mentioned in the said Schedule form the basis of this contract, and if there shall be any untrue statement or misrepresentation in such proposal or declaration, then this Policy shall be void and all moneys paid in respect hereof shall be forfeit to the Association.

(2) That the premium or premiums be duly paid to the Association, as stated in the Schedule, and no payment of money shall be binding on the Association, unless in exchange for the Association's official receipt signed by the Manager or Secretary. This Policy shall not be in force until the first premium has been paid. All succeeding premiums must be paid within one calendar month after the date specified in the Schedule, otherwise the Policy will cease to be in force, but it may be revived within twelve months after the said date, subject to the Directors being satisfied as to the continued good health of the Life Assured, and on payment of the premium or premiums in arrear with interest thereon at the rate of 5 per cent per annum. Should death occur within the aforesaid one calendar month, and before payment of the premium, the sum assured will be payable under deduction of the said premium. In the event of the age of the Life Assured having been understated, the Policy shall not become void, but such sum only shall be paid hereunder as would have been assured or the premium actually received if the age had been correctly stated. Proof of age must be given before any claim hereunder can be admitted.

(3) That the Life Assured shall not, without licence previously obtained from the Association, engage in any naval or military service except as a member of the Auxiliary Forces in the United Kingdom of Great Britain and Ireland, or in any seafaring occupation, or in trade in absolute liquors, or expose himself in any capacity to the risks of actual warfare.

(4) That the Life Assured shall not, without licence previously obtained from the Association, travel or reside in Asia, or south of 33 north latitude or north of 30 south latitude ; but may, without special licence, pass by sea over the prohibited area in a decked vessel whilst proceeding to a place of destination within the allowed area ; and may also, without such licence, visit Egypt as far south as the Second Cataract of the Nile, from 1st November to 1st April, and reside in the Island of Madeira. But the restriction of residence shall lapse after five years from the commencement of this Policy, provided the Life Assured shall during such period have resided continuously within the free limit ; that he has attained the age of thirty ; and is not in military or seafaring occupation.

(5) That this Policy shall be void and all premiums forfeited to the Association, if the Life Assured shall, within two years of the date of the Policy, die by his or her own hands whether sane or insane, or by duelling, or by the hands of justice ; but without prejudice to the interests of other parties being bona fide onerous holders.

SCHEDULE.

Name, Address, and Calling of the Life Assured.	James Arthur Browne, of No. 10 Russell Square, London, W.C. Medical Practitioner
Name, Address, and Calling of the person in whose favour the Assurance is granted.	The Same
Date of Proposal and Declaration, and by whom made.	The Twenty-seventh day of December, one thousand eight hundred and ninety-seven — The Same.
Date of birth stated in Proposal.	The Twenty-eighth day of December, one thousand eight hundred and sixty-five.
Sum assured, Table, and if with or without profits,	Four hundred and seventy-six pounds and five shillings (£476:5:0) Table LA., with Profits
When sum assured payable.	Immediately on satisfactory proof of the death above named. of James Arthur Browne, and of the title of the person claiming payment.
To whom sum assured is payable.	The Executors, Administrators, or Assigns of the said James Arthur Browne.
Premium.	Twelve pounds and ten shillings (£12:10:0)
Due Date of premium each year,	The Twenty-seventh day of December.
Period during which premium is payable.	During the life of the said James Arthur Browne.
Special Provisions (if any).	None.

Age admitted
7.11.1900.

SIGNED and SEALED with the Seal of the Association at Edinburgh this Seventeenth day of January One thousand eight hundred and ninety eight.

Entered

Examined

Director.

Secretary.

Director.

No Notice of Assignment or other Notice affecting this Policy will be valid unless delivered to the Head Office of the Association, No. 24 YORK PLACE, EDINBURGH.

main provincial cities as far south as Portsmouth, with one branch in Wales at Cardiff.

In addition to the special new schemes in the sickness and accident department the company had taken powers to write public liability and fidelity guarantee risks. It was in these two classes that the company incurred the penalty of moving too fast without adequate experience. In order to build up premium income, public liability risks such as those of horse-tram and steam-tram operators were written, not only in Scotland, but in many parts of England and Wales. In the year 1888 claims on these risks, together with five fatal accident claims, resulted in a heavy loss on the year's trading. In the ensuing economy drive James Black offered to reduce his own salary of £300 per annum by £85. This was declined but the directors held him responsible for much that had gone wrong, and his resignation was accepted in April 1889. Following his departure the consultant actuary John Deuchar reported that James Black had taken with him the actuarial tables and other important documents, but when pressed he returned them.

There then emerged two men who, under a strong board, were to set the company on a firm course. The first, Henry Brown, a draper in Manchester, was one of the earliest and most successful of the agents appointed in 1885. Two years later he had been appointed superintendent of agents for all the English branches other than those in the four northernmost counties which were supervised from Edinburgh head office, together with the Scottish branches, by Andrew Young, appointed superintendent of agents in 1887. As station-master of the Highland Railway at Elgin he had had no insurance experience other than that of a part-time agent of the company in Morayshire before assuming this appointment.

Henry Brown came to Edinburgh as manager in 1889, starting his 29-year term as chief executive and Andrew Young was appointed secretary, a post which he was to hold until 1914. The ability and initiative of these two men set the policy which was to carry forward the company on an aggressive course of development unchecked over the next 25 years, both in the UK and overseas, until progress was slowed down by the outbreak of war in 1914. Working with them was John Little who was the first office boy in 1885, and who, before his retirement in 1933, was to hold the appointments of secretary and, finally, general manager of The Century. He was elected a director after his retirement.

It was a difficult position with which the directors were faced in 1889. The non-cancellable sickness scheme, which had been acclaimed by the market from its introduction in 1885, was still weighed down by the heavy loadings imposed by the actuary in his valuation of the fund. A firm base was needed. Henry Brown set himself the task of reducing

Andrew Young, secretary and John Macdonald, claims manager

expenses by 25 per cent and increasing the premium income by 50 per cent after pruning the accident risks extensively. This he achieved, but claims continued to come in, and the Directors' Reports for the next four years continued to emphasise the need for cutting down expenses. By the end of 1891 the situation had improved to an extent which allowed the first dividend of 4 per cent to be paid on the shares, and the directors, who for the first five years had not drawn any fees, accepted 125 gns between the seven of them. Gradual growth continued and in 1893 the sickness fund which had stood at £1,758 in 1889 had increased to more than £14,000. By the end of 1895 the figure stood at £32,000.

The sickness and accident policy gained favour with the medical, legal and other professional classes for whom it was designed. Selection was strict and a high proportion of proposals were declined. The question of accepting females was raised as early as 1891 and as an experiment three females were covered at rates of premium normal for the permanent contract, but giving cover only on an annual basis. In 1897 an accidents-only scheme was devised for hospital nurses, but it was more than 50 years later that the non-cancellable policy was freely offered to women in the professions.

In 1888, on the suggestion of the Aberdeen directors, the company took over the Fidelity, Accident, Sickness & General Assurance

'Good Samaritan' seal adopted by the Sickness and Accident Assurance Association in 1885, still used by The Century in The Phoenix Group 1982

Association Ltd of Aberdeen, a small but sound local company typical of many operating in those days. Later, in 1896, an agreement with the Northern Provident & Guarantee Society of Aberdeen to handle the society's reinsurance commitments was followed by that society being taken over in 1898, when the company felt more confident to handle larger risks in general insurance. Both of these subsidiaries were subsequently wound up.

By 1897, after 10 years' trading, the actuary was able to recommend the first payments on the sickness and accident policies of survival bonuses at age 65. In the same year R. M. M. Roddick, FFA, was appointed to be the first resident actuary. Powers were taken to write life business on the basis that 90 per cent of profits should go to the policyholders and 10 per cent to the shareholders. A deposit of £20,000 had to be made with the Court of Chancery. The name of the company was changed to the Sickness Accident & Life Association Ltd. In the new articles the company was empowered to write sickness, liability and fidelity guarantee risks but not fire, burglary or other accident risks. There was a board decision not to take on workmen's compensation risks at the rates then ruling for this cover then being introduced. The policy of the directors was to concentrate on the long term business and £10,000 was transferred from the sickness fund. A new issue of 10,200 shares was made, and from the premium obtained a further £10,000 was transferred to the life fund.

By 1899 the company, with funds of over £100,000 for the first time, and with an investment reserve of £5,000, had achieved a measure of stability and was able to pay a dividend of 15 per cent to shareholders. By 1901 the chairman, John Campbell Lorimer, reported favourably on the strength of the sickness fund and the shareholders agreed to adopt a less cumbersome name. In the euphoria of the new year they happily changed it to The Century Insurance Company Ltd. After completion of the first five years of the life account in the following year the actuary, R. M. M. Roddick, recommended a reversionary bonus of £1 10s 0d per cent with an interim rate of £1 per cent, the shareholders' dividend being raised from 15 per cent to 17½ per cent.

Over the next five years Henry Brown developed successfully a policy of expansion in the general insurance field in the UK so generating funds for the further development of the strongly based life and PHI accounts. In 1904 the capital of the company was increased again and fire and burglary insurance accounts were opened. The London market in those days led on a high proportion of the major fire risks in the USA, but after the disasters in 1906 of the San Francisco fire, and the earthquake and subsequent fires in Valparaiso and Santiago, Henry Brown assured agents that The Century was not involved in any risks outside the United Kingdom. There were, indeed, outward signs of the company's prosperity to be seen in the opening of new premises for the company's branches at 27 Queen Victoria Street in the City of London and also in Leeds, Manchester and Glasgow, and the first Irish branch at Belfast, all in 1906. These followed the acquisition in 1904 of the fine office at 18 Charlotte Square in Edinburgh which was to be the headquarters of The Century for the next 70 years. The price paid for that building was £8,000, and its funding was assisted by a mortgage loan of £1,000 taken from the Great Western Laundry Company of Glasgow.

The company's interest in general insurance was further expanded in 1907 when the Mutual Guarantee Company Ltd (named originally the Friendly Societies and General Guarantee Company Ltd 1876–96) was taken over, bringing in a fire and accident premium income of approximately £10,000 (£5,000 in the fire department) which was roughly the same volume as that then being written by The Century. The plate glass section of the Mutual Guarantee business, however, was not profitable and it was decided to hive this off in 1908 to a newly formed subsidiary called the Southern Insurance Company Ltd. The Century was by now a fully fledged composite office and, although it was small, reports in the press and elsewhere show that it was very well respected throughout the UK, especially in Scotland. It operated as a tariff company, being a member of both the Fire Offices' Committee and the Accident Offices' Association.

In 1907 and 1908 two events led to The Century starting its overseas account which was to become a major feature of its subsequent development. The first was an approach by Thomas Langlois, president of the Pacific Coast Fire Insurance Company of Vancouver BC. He knew of The Century as a leader in the Guarantee Bond market in Edinburgh and offered to write a fire account for The Century in Western Canada. Henry Brown's advice to the board was that 'unless The Century was to "keep clear" of the colonial field for all time it seemed a favourable opportunity for a tentative trial'. He thought the difficulties of direct writing in Canada would be too great to contemplate. It was this beginning, followed by the acquisition in 1920 of the shares of the Pacific Coast Fire, which gave The Century its first overseas interest other than agency connections.

The second major event was a call at 18 Charlotte Square by Henry I. Brown of Philadelphia, Pennsylvania, who was so intrigued by the similarity between his name and that of the general manager of The Century that he invited proposals from The Century to take a share of reinsurance through his family company, Henry W. Brown & Company in Philadelphia and New York. Henry Brown of The Century visited the USA and Canada in 1908, and after an initial underwriting agreement there was established a direct share in the business of Henry W. Brown & Company, writing in most states in the USA. This was to become the biggest single item in The Century world-wide fire and accident portfolio, continuing until the formation of the USA branch in 1930. As Henry Brown's confidence in the overseas market grew, a portfolio of foreign business written in London was started in 1910; and agencies were established between then and 1914 in Holland, Belgium, France, Germany, Austria, Denmark, Norway and Switzerland in Europe, and elsewhere at Sydney, Brisbane, Rangoon, Bombay and Calcutta. The Anglo-Scottish Insurance Company came under The Century management in 1912 and was fully taken over in 1914. From then on it shared with The Century the direct writing of fire business in Canada, under the management of the Pacific Coast Fire.

The story in the UK was one of steady progress. Although in the difficult conditions in 1900 and 1904 transfers had to be made from the life fund to meet depreciation in the invested assets, the funds grew by nearly tenfold from £136,000 in 1900 to £1,274,000 in 1914. Reports on the long term business in the life department and the PHI department showed steady growth coupled with a regular decrease in the expense ratio. The life bonus was kept at each quinquennium at the rate of £1 10s 0d per cent (with an interim rate of £1 5s 0d per cent) and the shareholders' dividend gradually rose from 15 per cent to 20 per cent. It was undoubtedly the initiative and inspiration of Henry Brown which brought success, but much credit must be given to the secretary, Andrew Young. R. M. M. Roddick, FFA, resident actuary since life business was

*18 Charlotte Square,
Edinburgh, head office of
The Century 1904–74*

*The boardroom,
18 Charlotte Square*

first written in 1897, retired in 1908 and was succeeded by Willie
Robertson, FFA, who was to become president of the Faculty of Actuaries
and the acknowledged leading authority in the UK on permanent health
insurance. The number of branches in the UK remained unchanged
except for the addition of a new branch in Dublin under the management
of Bill McConnell, previously with the Caledonian. He was an Irishman of
great charm and character who became associated with the Rotarian
movement when it was first brought from the United States to Ireland,
and was proud to hold the title of Rotarian No 1 in Europe. He remained
in Dublin until he was appointed the first manager of The Century USA
branch in New York in 1930.

Development continued to be concentrated on the long term business
and particularly on life schemes such as family income benefit and
education endowment policies. A very early form of house purchase
scheme for the public, and a pension scheme for The Century staff were

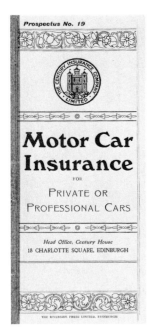

Motor prospectus
c 1920

well designed and well presented. In the general insurance department the company followed the lead of the tariff offices in each new development such as loss of profits, household policies and the changing form of employers' liability cover, continuing its specialist line in guarantee bonds.

Steady progress continued unchecked until the outbreak of war in August 1914. The firm management had the backing of a strong board led by Sheriff John Campbell Lorimer, KC, who, with J. B. Sutherland and two other directors, A. Peddie-Waddell and William Towers-Clark, guided the fortunes of the company from its foundation covering a period of more than 30 years. Andrew Young retired at the end of 1914 after 25 years as secretary and died in 1939 at the age of 93. He was succeeded as secretary by John Little. The only other leading executive was Willie Robertson, FFA, who had been appointed actuary in 1908. By the early years of the century the company was firmly established in the life, sickness and general insurance markets, predominantly in Scotland but also in London and the provinces. The Anglo-Scottish, in addition to its entry in Canada, was used by The Century in its cautious start to gain experience in both motor and marine insurance. The entry into the marine market met the call by London underwriters in 1914 to find capacity to replace lines formerly written in London by German and Austrian insurers. Fire treaty arrangements with German companies also had to be cancelled when, in September 1914, it became illegal to trade with the enemy. The Century took a full share in the early days of writing air raid insurance, a risk which like the war risk in marine policies was subsequently taken over by the Government, leaving the insurance market to handle the business on a commission basis, which

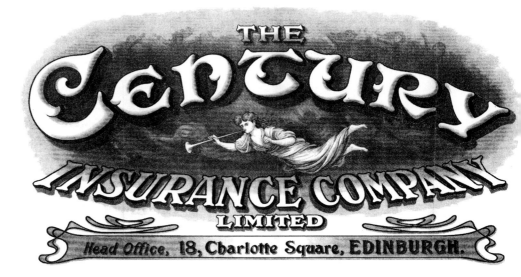

Century life policy
heading, 1909

in the event proved very profitable. Unsuccessful attempts to take over the Sceptre Life Association Ltd of London were made in July 1914, and again in 1917, when the Sceptre was taken over by the Eagle Star.

Despite the check on life and PHI in all departments, underwriting and investment results were consistently satisfactory throughout the difficult conditions of war. It was a matter of proper pride that after the quinquennial valuation of the life fund in 1917 the actuary, Willie Robertson, was able to recommend the payment of a reversionary bonus of £1 5s 0d per cent, reducing the 1902–12 rate by only 5s 0d per cent.

In the meantime however the situation at the head office of The Century was moving towards a major change. Two of the original directors died, and Henry Brown was elected to the board in 1916. He was by this time aged 60, and behind him there were only John Little, secretary, aged 48 and Willie Robertson, the actuary, aged 40, neither of whom at that time was regarded as strong enough to succeed as general manager. The board therefore was ready to accept a bid for the shares of the company and the story of how this was negotiated in January 1918 with Friends' Provident Institution has already been told in the last chapter. War-time conditions certainly made it difficult to find the right personality to ensure the continuing independence of this proud and successful Scottish company, but it was a great surprise to the market that the board accepted a bid from a small, little known, Quaker-controlled provincial mutual life office, with no branch organisation, and no executives of any stature other than Henry Tapscott and Alfred Moorhouse. Friends' Provident Institution at that time was writing a restricted, albeit very profitable, life account approximately half the size of that of The Century, with no sickness or general insurance account. Many of the staff of The Century who were absent on war service were undoubtedly shocked when the news was conveyed to them. The future, however, was to show that the best of them were to take leading roles in Henry Tapscott's plans for the combined Friends' Provident and Century Life Office. These were worked out in a manner which ensured that the company never lost its individuality, or its Scottish head office, throughout more than 50 years, during which both Friends' Provident and The Century enjoyed the mutual advantages of the merger.

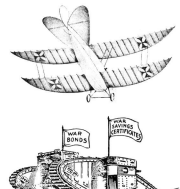

TOP *Air Raid Personal Accident prospectus, World War I*

ABOVE *War Bond Scheme Policy prospectus World War I*

Chapter 4

Growth with The Century
1919~39

ALTHOUGH IN THE spring of 1918 the war was in its last and most critical phase, Henry Tapscott and Henry Brown set to work, using The Century branch organisation, on far-reaching plans to secure maximum advantage for both Friends' Provident and The Century by cultivating each other's connections. The Quaker directors ensured the preservation of the standards and character of FPI, and The Century's well-trained managers and staff provided the strength in head office and branches, which FPI could not have otherwise easily recruited.

First, life and annuity business, other than The Century combined life and sickness schemes, would in future be written by Friends' Provident. Secondly, control of a vigorous development programme for The Century general business would be centred in London, linking it more closely with both national and international markets in which expansion had to be sought. The Century in this way left the ranks of the fine Scottish offices which had contributed greatly to standards of insurance in the UK, but was to find its place amongst the most respected general offices in London.

For Friends' Provident agents Henry Tapscott's plans brought just what they had been denied for so long. Even though the new series of policies since 1903 did not carry bonuses so favourable as those paid prior to that date, the terms were competitive and they could work with The Century branch managers in developing non-Friend connections. The actuary, Alfred Moorhouse, was a man of vision but was not yet ready to introduce some generally accepted developments in the life schemes offered; in particular he was slow to see the future potential of

7 Leadenhall Street, EC3.
London head office
1928–74

57

Alfred Moorhouse,
actuary

pension scheme business. It was inevitably an uphill task to introduce to clients, with no broker support such as later generations had, a new and lengthy name to compete with well established companies in a very conservative market. Nevertheless much was achieved and the record of new sums assured crept slowly up through the '20s from £1.331 million in 1920 to £1.846 million in 1930, but fell back again during the years of the Depression.

The industrial and economic climate of those years held difficulties which included the coal strike in 1920, the General Strike in May 1926, and in the City, after a short return to the gold standard, Britain was forced to abandon it in 1931. It was a tough time for any life salesman and for general insurance business prospects were no better.

The Century fire account in the UK grew steadily and profitably under Harold Sutcliffe. Quaker industrial and commercial connections brought new sources of premium income, sometimes secured for The Century by

*The General Strike 1926.
City workers travel to
work on a steam traction-
engine and trailer in
Cornhill*
BBC HULTON PICTURE
LIBRARY

a mortgage or debenture loan from Friends' Provident. With a head office
in London the company was able to take part more easily in the
reinsurance market and long-lasting and profitable connections were
built up with companies such as Sterling Offices, Swiss Re, Copenhagen
Re and Munich Re. The Century was also one of the six founder
shareholders of Treaty Reinsurances Ltd, of which Dr Cecil Golding was
manager and Henry Tapscott had a seat on the board. The volume of
direct fire business was increased substantially when the Liverpool
Marine & General Insurance Co Ltd was taken over in 1926.

On the accident side The Century in Edinburgh had a strong personal
sickness and accident department but had been slow to expand in the
liability field, possibly influenced by its unfortunate experience in the
early days. There was no Century man to manage this department, and
Herbert Rowntree, a Yorkshire Friend whose experience had been with
the Alliance, was appointed manager after his war service with a
Friends' Ambulance Unit. He was author of a standard textbook on Third
Party Insurance, and his apparent over-caution concealed an aptitude
for tackling the unusual risk such as film producers' indemnity, and the
emerging hazards of the rapidly growing motor insurance market,
particularly following the introduction of compulsory motor insurance
by the Road Traffic Act in 1930. During this period new hazards called
for underwriting skill in both the third party and employers' liability
sections. In 1919 The Century participated with 35 other offices of the
Accident Offices' Association in forming the Aircraft Accident Pool, but
when in 1926 the aviation company market developed The Century was

*John Little, general
manager and secretary,
The Century*

not able to find a place as shareholder in one of the two companies
formed jointly by the principal British composite companies until a
vacancy occurred in the Aviation and General in 1939. This was to
prove an interesting and profitable investment after the war, and the
A & G in 1972 was one of the first two British insurance companies to
receive the Queen's Award to Industry for export achievement. Overall it
was a constant struggle to maintain a profitable record in the accident
department in the '20s and '30s, but it was necessary to maintain the FP
& CLO's standing as a composite office if fire profits were to be maintained
and new life connections developed.

In the marine department The Century had great difficulty in the '20s.
From Edinburgh the account had been written by rather unsatisfactory
London managers. In 1922 Henry Tapscott placed the account in both
London and New York under the management of the Commercial Union.
This led to fluctuating fortune and the Office was precluded from writing

an independent marine account until the Liverpool Marine & General joined the group. The L M & G unfortunately brought a serious unrevealed loss in New York but they had two underwriters, Frank Hotine and Philip Freeborn, who established disciplines for The Century in both London and New York, and later elsewhere overseas, which ensured a profit for the marine department over the next 45 years in markets where changes of fortune were frequent and violent.

The long term business of The Century under the keen eye of Willie Robertson in Edinburgh continued to maintain profitable growth despite the setbacks which followed successive periods of economic recession and industrial unrest. The PHI policy held its unchallenged position in the market, but the only other long-term business written by The Century was in the combined life and sickness schemes, and a limited amount of sinking fund business.

One of the most impressive examples of Henry Tapscott's initiative was his introduction of hire purchase business to the London insurance market. He had been much impressed during his visit to the United States in 1933 by the rapidly growing motor car hire purchase business in which some American insurance companies had taken an interest. He put before the board a proposition for a new company to be called the Mutual Indemnity & Guarantee Corporation Ltd, but he advised that the shares of this company should not be held by The Century because he thought that this might excite undesirable notice in the insurance market. He explained that the venture was experimental, and that if it failed it would be embarrassing to have the name of The Century associated with it; and if on the other hand he achieved the success which he hoped for, he did not wish to attract the envious attention of other insurance companies. The initial shareholding of the company therefore was held by the managing director of the new company, Hector Tilley, who had experience in this field, together with three officials of The Century, Harry Hastings, Bernard Brigham and Charles Sutcliffe, and two members of the Mutual Indemnity staff. The trading experience was an immediate success and after two years the board was convinced that the Mutual Indemnity & Guarantee was sufficiently respectable for the shares to be acquired by The Century. Henry Tapscott, Alfred Moorhouse and Herbert Rowntree were appointed directors, so identifying the success of the new company with the FP & CLO.

By 1929 The Century accounts, especially in the USA and Canada, were growing at a pace which called for remittances greater than could be expected from the life fund. It was recalled that there had been criticism of the high proportion, at 15 per cent of the life fund, used to acquire The Century in 1918, so some source of market funds was sought. A holding company, Century Insurance Trust Limited, was

Harold Sutcliffe, assistant general manager

formed to hold the shares of all the general insurance subsidiaries and, through this company, finance on short-term debenture terms was brought in to fund development particularly for the subsidiary companies in overseas markets.

By 1928 the London head office at 42 Kingsway was outgrown, so a newly built office at 7 Leadenhall Street in the City was acquired. This brought all departments into closer touch with the insurance and investment markets in the City. The management was strengthened by the appointment of Harold Sutcliffe as assistant general manager, and Harry Daniel added the duties of fire manager to those of overseas manager, with Herbert Rowntree continuing in charge of the accident department.

Looking back over the '20s there was good reason for satisfaction with the progress made by FP & CLO since the move from Bradford, and the board decided in 1930 that instead of waiting for the next normal quinquennial year in 1934 a special centenary bonus should be declared in 1932, and at the same time the Office should change from the normal quinquennial period to a triennial valuation and declaration of bonus. Even though the black clouds of the Depression were already over America, its devastating effect on the economy of the world was not fully foreseen in Europe or the Commonwealth. Much has been written about the suddenness of the shock of the Depression which first struck the United States in 1929. The complete evaporation of confidence brought economic paralysis throughout the country, largely due to the instability, at that time, of the small-unit state based banking system in

*Traffic congestion
Leadenhall Street –
Gracechurch Street,
London EC3, 1925*
POPPERFOTO

the USA. A very large number of banks were closed and many general insurance companies wound up. In 1931, Henry Tapscott reported that a large American insurance company had been asked to allow payment of salaries in cash in the company's office, rather than through the bank, in order to avoid the impression given by insurance clerks being seen in the bank withdrawing money. The country was ill prepared for the catastrophe when it came. Ruin faced those whose way of life was built on loans and hire purchase agreements; homes were abandoned and there was no form of property which could be expected to maintain its value. The situation was made very much worse by the decline in moral values which had spread through the country like a plague as the result of the failure of the XVIIIth Amendment of the Constitution which had introduced Prohibition in 1920, and opened the door to the rogue and racketeer.

In Canada where neither the banking system nor the liquor laws held the same difficulties, the Depression came more slowly, but inevitably dependence on close alliance with the American economy brought the slump both to the industrial areas of Ontario, British Columbia and Quebec and also to the under-financed farmers in the Prairies, where the oil wealth of Alberta had not yet been discovered. In other major overseas territories where The Century was represented, the Depression took its toll. In countries like Australia, South Africa and India, primary producers were very largely dependent on the prosperity of world-wide markets, particularly those in the UK.

In the investment department the gross yield on the life fund had been

63

*Bernard Brigham,
secretary*

commendably raised from £5 7s 11d per cent in 1919 to £6 1s 4d per cent in 1930 but much of this had been achieved by investing more widely than other life companies in Canada and US dollar investments. When the crash came the FP & CLO percentage of depreciation on dollar investments was more than twice that of its competitors. The overall depreciation was over 50 per cent. It came as a staggering blow, when underwriting results were running so badly in 1929 and 1930, to have to face in addition investment depreciation unprecedented in the insurance industry.

In June 1931 Henry Tapscott had to report a critical situation in New York, and in the UK difficult trading and investment conditions were giving cause for concern. Heavy falls in premium income forced the Office to take extreme measures to counter the rise in expense ratios. In the New York branch, which had only been set up in January 1930, staff was reduced by 27 per cent in 1932 and all expenses were cut back. In the UK new life premium income decreased by 55 per cent, largely due to the fall in single premium and annuity business, which had been sought to accumulate funds for investment. The general premium income of

The Century fell by 25 per cent over the two years 1929 and 1930. It was a time when work was hard to get and rewards were small, and the security of a job in insurance was keenly sought and jealously held. In 1931, conforming with the action taken by many employers at that time, salaries of the majority of the staff in the UK were reduced by 10 per cent and the directors accepted a similar cut in their own fees. The total UK staff numbered 425 but 130 with salaries under £100 per annum were not affected by this reduction so the total saving achieved was only £10,000 per annum. In the United States and Canada 10 per cent cuts were imposed on all salaries in excess of $400 per annum, and similar measures were taken in South Africa, Australia and India. It was not until 1934 that these cuts in salaries were cancelled or any general improvements in salary levels were awarded.

At the end of 1931 the assets of the Office fell short of liabilities by 5.3 per cent on the total of £7,276,000, very largely reflecting the situation in USA and Canada, but it was decided to make no transfer from the life fund to correct the situation until the results of the 1932 valuation were known. The directors had to decide, however, that the resolutions passed in 1930 for a special centenary bonus in 1932, and for subsequent triennial valuations, would have to be cancelled. They looked forward to the next normal valuation year in 1934 with confidence which was justified by events, but the decade beyond that was to bring again the horrors of war.

As the Depression moved slowly away during the years 1933–34 it was a struggle for the Office to recover the momentum to support the policy of expansion for both Friends' Provident and The Century, even with the help of the composite branch organisation, and with The Century enjoying closer links with the London markets for development of general insurance. Brokers were reluctant to switch from old friends. Solicitors and accountants were closely linked to the major composite companies through the appointment of local directors. The restrictive regulations of the Fire Offices' Committee denied the appointment by The Century of a director from any professional firm or bank in which another member of the FOC had made an appointment. It was not until 1942 that a change in the Friends' Provident Rules permitted the appointment of non-Friends as local directors of the life office. In Scotland however, where the old Century connections were well established, the FP & CLO was able to use them. One device, however, was employed by Henry Tapscott in the '30s. He took advantage of the fact that the registered office of The Century was still in Edinburgh, and this enabled him to appoint a London Advisory Board for The Century. This attracted business for both Friends' Provident and The Century through the influence of English local directors of The Century, meeting in London.

Harold Morland,
chairman

Investment policy

Henry Tapscott's keen interest in investment matters led to emphasis on the use of investment policy as a means of securing both life and general premium income. The Office had for many years operated an attractive house purchase loan scheme which brought in a volume of life business and profitable household general business. A very successful professional loan scheme, devised by Henry Tapscott, for helping doctors, dentists, solicitors and accountants to purchase their practices brought not only personal business but very favourable publicity and agency support. It was, however, in the field of large mortgage loans, or unquoted debentures for industrial and commercial companies, that the greatest source of premium income was found. Under the terms of these loans all the insurances of the borrowers were tied to the office, and a useful personal insurance connection was also secured. There were many famous names amongst the borrowers in this category and two instances

66

will illustrate how valuable service to the borrower brought a substantial connection to the Office. Participation in a debenture loan made by a consortium of insurance companies to the Inveresk Group of paper mills and publishers made in the '20s led to the Office sharing in what looked like a disaster for Inveresk in 1933. The other participating insurance companies would not follow Henry Tapscott's lead to see the company through the Depression. He took over their shares of the debenture raising the Office's commitment to nearly £100,000, a very big sum in those days, and enabled Inveresk to pull through the crisis. In return the Office retained for more than 30 years one of its important life and general business connections. The other case was that of Josiah Wedgwood & Sons Ltd, the famous family pottery company, which, after the crisis of the Depression, found themselves in 1937 forced by subsidence resulting from coal-mining to abandon the site where they had operated for nearly 180 years. The then managing director, the Hon Josiah Wedgwood, came to the City to finance a very courageous scheme for building a new factory at Barlaston five miles outside Stoke-on-Trent. With profits averaging only £25,000 per annum he was looking for finance initially at £150,000. The Office arranged this, and maintained a very happy association with Wedgwood over the next 40 years, becoming the largest shareholder in the outstandingly successful public company developed by the Hon Josiah Wedgwood, and later under the chairmanship of Sir Arthur Bryan. Inevitably there were some investments in this category which got into difficulty during World War II, but losses were very few, and many of the profitable general insurance connections secured by The Century led also to an open door for Friends' Provident when branch managers were seeking outlets for the pension scheme business which was to become a main feature of the Office's development programme.

The Century symbol used on notepaper and sales literature

During these years of peace between the wars the Office enjoyed satisfactory mortality experience although not of course as favourable as that of the Quaker membership prior to 1915. For the 1934 valuation Alfred Moorhouse adopted the new tables of mortality known as the A1924-29 prepared jointly by the Institute of Actuaries in England and the Faculty of Actuaries in Scotland, and was able to report that the mortality experience of the Office was substantially better than that of the average expected by these tables. The rate of interest assumed was 3 per cent, with the average rate earned during that quinquennium being £4 11s 10d per cent net. The gross rate of interest increased to £6 1s 4d per cent in 1930, but that was the peak. The effect of Britain coming off the gold standard in 1931, and the subsequent conversion of War Loan (from 5 per cent to 3½ per cent) brought the gross rate down to £4 17s 11d per cent in 1932. It was not for another quarter of a century that the rate of interest was again raised above 6 per cent even in the years when The Century was contributing substantial PHI and general insurance profits which were a major factor in the gross yield on the FP & CLO life fund. At the time of the 1924 valuation the Friends' Provident investment in The Century of £560,000 produced a dividend yield of £4 9s 7d per cent. By 1934 this investment, increased to £1m, gave a yield of £6 2s 0d per cent over the quinquennium.

When Alfred Moorhouse submitted his last valuation that year it was not possible to match the record rate for the FP & CLO reversionary bonus of £2 2s 0d per cent declared in 1929, but it was a mark of the strength of the Office in the prevailing conditions that the rate was £1 15s 0d per cent for both the reversionary and interim bonuses. The confidence shown by the directors by this declaration was to be shattered by war before the quinquennium ended, and the next declaration had to be deferred until the end of World War II, based on the 10 years to 31st December 1944. In the meantime, however, optimism prevailed in the development plans worked out for Friends' Provident and for The Century in both UK and overseas branches.

No form of indulgence accords readily with the tenets of the Society of Friends, and in the year when the proposal for a special bonus had to be deferred, and when the majority of salaries and the directors' fees had been cut by 10 per cent, there was little to encourage a mood for centenary celebrations. There was, however, published a small pamphlet entitled *One Hundred Years of the Friends' Provident* written by Arthur Rowntree to whom the authors of this book acknowledge their debt.

When John Little, general manager and secretary of The Century, retired in 1933, he was elected to The Century board leaving Willie Robertson the actuary as the sole survivor of the senior executives of The Century from pre-merger days. This gave Henry Tapscott the opportunity to carry out the concentration in London of the majority of the executive and administrative functions of The Century and its subsidiary companies. The accounts other than those of the Edinburgh head office were transferred to London into the care of Bernard Brigham, FCA, then an assistant general manager. The investments which had been the special care of John Little were also transferred to London where Charles Bosanquet from Lazard Bros had recently been appointed assistant general manager (investments). In the department the senior official was Miss Margery Chuter who was to have the distinction of being the first lady to be appointed investment secretary of a British life office, and with her vivacious assistant, Miss Millicent Black (Mrs C. Little) she earned for the Office the affectionate nickname of 'The Girls' Friendly Society'.

As the overseas business of The Century had been concentrated in

Harry Daniel, assistant general manager

London since 1920 this left in Edinburgh head office the supervision of the Scottish branches of the general departments, and for the UK as a whole, of the very important PHI department (then known as the continuous disability department) under the firm control of the actuary, Willie Robertson, who jealously guarded his preserves, resenting any challenge of his decisions from London head office or branches. By later standards the PHI department was small with a premium income which grew from £35,000 in 1932 to £47,000 in 1939 but it was a very profitable account, producing transfers to the profit and loss account of £20,000 at each of the quinquennial valuations in this period, and building up reserves which were to prove very welcome contributions to The Century dividend in later years. The continuing success of this specialist department was rightly a matter of pride in the Edinburgh head office, where it was to be controlled for a further 40 years.

At the AGM in May 1936 Alfred Moorhouse, actuary since 1904 and actuary and secretary since 1924, handed over his appointments, being succeeded on the actuarial side by John Robson, and on the secretarial side by Bernard Brigham. He had completed 50 years' service with Friends' Provident and was elected to the board, on which he served for a further 12 years. His retirement severed the last major link with the great characters who had built up the FPI in Bradford in the 19th century. Under the tutelage of his two eminent predecessors, Joseph Dymond and John Tennant, he was the first actuary of the FPI to qualify by examination as a Fellow of the Institute of Actuaries. He had shown strength of character and high principle in his professional guidance of the Office for 32 years.

Alfred Moorhouse's successor as actuary, John Robson, was also a link with the past and was to make, over the next 20 years, a comparable contribution in supporting the general managers with whom he served. It was to be a very difficult period in which the FP & CLO would be struggling, through the difficulties of war and the problems of the post-war period, to establish its claim for a place amongst the leading British offices. John Robson had joined The Century in Edinburgh in 1907 and after service in the Army came back to find that he had been 'taken over with the furniture' in the merger with FPI. He was soon marked down amongst the ablest young men in Edinburgh head office and was brought to London in 1923. When Alfred Moorhouse's assistant, Finlay Cameron, resigned to become general manager of his old company, the Caledonian, it was thus again a Century man to whom Henry Tapscott was able to turn for the strength needed to take Friends' Provident forward.

A feature of the first new schemes which John Robson introduced was his emphasis on the non-profit policy with the addition of family income benefit which, in a period of low interest rates, was being developed in the

Henry Tapscott with Association Football team 1931, winners of Insurance Minor Cup

market. His biggest contribution, however, to the future development of the FP & CLO was to bring the Office to the fore in the ranks of British life offices handling group life and pensions business. This market was stimulated at that time by the withdrawal from London of the Metropolitan Life of New York, leaving the demand for this type of scheme far from satisfied. With little enthusiasm from Alfred Moorhouse, Friends' Provident had first started writing pensions business in 1934 and by John Robson's second year in 1937 the volume being handled was sufficient for a separate group life and pensions department to be started under James Muir. By 1942 the department was credited with 33 per cent of the total new sums assured written, and in the following year nearly 45 per cent. In the post-war years during a period of rapid development in the ordinary life account the group life department was able to claim an average of 40 per cent or more of the total new life sums assured even in an era of frustration caused by constant changes in government regulations affecting company pension schemes.

It was not only in the volume of new business written that the group life department played its part. Its success was probably the biggest single factor in bringing the name of Friends' Provident to the notice of the public. A steadily growing number of employers, with their staff and pensioners, came to realise the value of the service which the Office was providing. The development of pensions business also did much to build up the Office's connections with those brokers, large and small, who, after the introduction of the National Insurance Scheme in 1948, were specialising in advising employers on insured pensions for their staff.

From the time he took over as actuary John Robson had very able assistance from Harold Cope, FIA, as assistant actuary until he was transferred in 1943 to be assistant general manager in charge of investments. Cope was succeeded by Dennis Jackson, FIA, who was later to follow Robson as actuary. The late '30s, with a mounting threat of war, were difficult times for any forward planning but the staff responded well to the strong leadership of Henry Tapscott, and there emerged a new generation of branch managers, amongst whom the outstanding characters were Geoffrey Seabrooke, the brothers Bill and George Palmer and Godfrey Goodbody. They and others were to prove their strength in guiding both Friends' Provident and The Century in the post-war years.

During this period the Office first made its appearance as the owner of substantial office buildings in provincial cities. Starting with a new building at 37–39 Corn Street, Bristol, with a façade by Sir Giles Gilbert Scott, the office surveyor, A. W. Roques, FRIBA, also designed the fine building Century House, St Peter's Square, Manchester, and Century House, South Parade, Leeds.

A new Irish Insurance Act in 1936 provided that no office, other than domesticated companies, could be licensed to write both life and general insurance business. The majority of the big British composites decided to write general business and dispose of their life accounts. Godfrey Goodbody, however, with understanding of his fellow countrymen, was able to establish that Friends' Provident and The Century were quite separate in their identities, and so each could continue on its own ground. The Norwich Union Society took the same line. This decision brought mixed fortune for the Office over the next 34 years; The Century experienced many years of very heavy losses until it was finally withdrawn altogether in 1970. Friends' Provident on the other hand achieved great success in the Republic, partly because of reduced competition after the withdrawal of British competitors.

In the later years of the '30s the policy of the Office was to resume the vigorous expansion which had been checked by the Depression. Henry Tapscott's investment policy and John Robson's pension scheme business were the two main features in the increase of the new life sums assured from £1.5 million in 1932 to the peak figure of £2.7 million in 1937. This record was not passed until 1946, the first full year after World War II.

Century Insurance Building, St Peter's Square, Manchester

The development of general insurance overseas is described in Appendix II. In the UK expansion was not spectacular but profits were made by strict selection and underwriting with fire claims ratios at a tolerable level of 45–55 per cent. The tariff companies had not as yet been seriously challenged on major risks by non-tariff companies and Lloyd's, but the growth of motor insurance after the Road Traffic Act 1930 brought keen competition from new companies and inexperienced brokers. It was not surprising that losses emerged before underwriters realised the potential dangers in motor claims. In the employers' liability and third party sections, too, claims were increasing relentlessly.

The marine account in London, mostly managed by the Commercial Union, although the Liverpool Marine & General wrote a small volume, suffered in the '30s severe fluctuations throughout a decade of considerable difficulty for the whole marine market. The risks were growing in size. When the *Queen Mary* was launched in 1935 the insurance cover required at £2.5 million was all placed in the London marine market stretching it to its fullest extent; and even this was only achieved by the government passing an Act enabling reinsurance cover to be provided by the state. Frank Hotine accepted for The Century his biggest ever line of £15,000; and when three years later the *Queen Elizabeth* was laid down £3 million out of a total of £4.5 million was the maximum placed in London The Century line was increased to £20,000. These figures seem small indeed when compared with the magnitude of later marine risks and the vast sums insured in the aviation market.

In the UK branches, following the practice of the time, the manager's function, other than administration and training, was largely the introduction of new business or the handling of complaints or difficulties with agents. All but the simplest of underwriting and claims settlements were handled in head office in London, managed by Harry Daniel in the fire department, and by Herbert Rowntree with his team of technicians in the accident department. In 1952, however, two agency superintendents were appointed, Jack Tranter in the fire department and Bob Nightingale on the accident side. By touring the country they kept branches in touch with the underwriting departments, and extended the branch manager's authority where possible. Both of these superintendents were to play an important part in the development of The Century, particularly overseas, after World War II.

Chapter 5

Wartime Conditions in the UK 1939~45

THE TRUE MENACE of Hitler's Germany was too slowly realised in England. In four years, he had overrun the Saar in 1935, re-militarised the German western border on the Rhine in 1936, and walked into Austria in the early months of 1938. When he claimed the German-speaking Sudetenland of Czechoslovakia in September 1938 the move was challenged by Britain and France, but they were sadly without the arms, strategic plans or indeed the resolution needed to stop this aggression. Neville Chamberlain and Edouard Daladier signed the Munich agreement in September 1938 heralding 'peace in our time', but the two countries were committed to declare war if Germany made any further encroachment on her neighbours. Less than a year later the German attack on Poland brought about the declaration of war on 3rd September 1939.

For the Office the first trial move was made in September 1938 when many members of the RNVR, TA and RAFVR were mobilised during the Munich crisis. In the expectation of air raids over London, sections of the staff from Leadenhall Street were dispersed for two weeks to work in two properties which the Office had taken over from defaulting mortgagors, a block of flats at Kings Court, Hammersmith and another property being developed at Grove Avenue, Sutton. The latter was to become familiar to many members of the staff who found their homes there after the war. From then on the staff were involved in various forms of training which were organised to meet the threat of bombs, incendiaries or gas. They attended First Aid and other Air Raid Precautions lectures, both in the Office and under local authority arrangements at home.

The Spirit of Defiance and Survival – looking from Cannon Street to St Paul's
BBC HULTON PICTURE LIBRARY

Major institutions in the City and Central London made arrangements during the early months of 1939 for moving their staff out of London, and an illustrated feature of *The Policy* in December that year shows an interesting selection of the country mansions and other buildings which were purchased for this purpose by insurance offices. The solution for the FP & CLO was the purchase early in 1939 of $7\frac{1}{2}$ acres at Harpenden adjacent to the home of the secretary, Bernard Brigham, and the erection of four large wooden huts built to the design of the office surveyor, Antoine Roques. As a safe and practical solution these huts proved to be a very satisfactory home for head office throughout the six years of war and continued in use for a further 12 years afterwards. Before the huts were ready, a large property called The Red House at Harpenden was acquired in the spring of 1939, and in May the mechanised section of the accounts department and their records were moved out there from City Gate House, Finsbury Circus. Two other properties, 6 and 8 Milton Road, Harpenden, were purchased for use partly as offices and partly as hostel accommodation. The plans prepared during the summer of 1939 involved arrangements for billets for 263 staff and 85 dependants at Harpenden.

The evacuation scheme provided for the majority of head office staff to work at Harpenden. This included the actuary, John Robson, with the life and pensions staff, Peter Leishman with the mortgage and property department, Samuel Mills, the deputy secretary, with the secretarial and administration sections; the accounts and their mechanised section had already been there since May. The underwriting and claims sections of the fire, accident and hire purchase departments also went to Harpenden and the whole organisation was under the direction of the secretary, Bernard Brigham, from his home next door to the hutted offices. The Office solicitor, John Shera Atkinson, took his staff to 9 Milton Road, Harpenden.

A small nucleus of the head office and City department staff was to remain at 7 Leadenhall Street where the general manager, Henry Tapscott, and the assistant general manager, Harold Sutcliffe, would spend most of the week. This ensured contact with the London and overseas markets and reinsurers and also the life and tariff committees. The investment department under Margery Chuter had to keep in touch with the Stock Exchange in London, and the marine department was to go with the Commercial Union manager to Ickenham, leaving two underwriters in the underground room in the old Lloyd's Building. The most important documents were to be stored by arrangement with Barclays Bank in strong rooms at Dunstable and Luton, the remainder being kept at 7 Leadenhall Street until a strong room could be built at Harpenden. In the event these plans worked well. Henry Tapscott's

circular 'What You Should Do In Case Of War' was sent out two weeks before the volunteer services were mobilised on 1st September 1939. With the prevalent fear of immediate and devastating air attack the staff were told to stay at home until they received instructions as to where and when to report for work, and they were given guidance as to what they should do if caught in an air raid. The summary of the circular starts with the sentence 'If the General Manager (or the government) declares a state of emergency, rota arrangements will come into force for work at Head Office and all Branches in neutral and evacuation areas'. It was actually the general manager who first declared a state of emergency on Tuesday, 28th August. Neville Chamberlain's announcement of the declaration of war was broadcast to the nation at 11.00 am the following Sunday, 3rd September; by which time the orderly move to Harpenden was well in hand. Amongst those who moved reluctantly and changed their way of life in 1939, there were several who were going to be equally reluctant to find themselves again on the treadmill of the commuter in 1945. 'For the duration', however, they walked or cycled to work and took their share of many civic duties called for by local Air Raid

Hut No 1 occupied by the accounts department at Harpenden, Herts in 1939

Herbert Rowntree with the Accident and the Southern Industrial Trust staff at Harpenden in the winter of 1940

Precautions, the National Fire Service, and the Home Guard. They settled into the social life of Harpenden and soon accepted, and were accepted by, their new community.

In London and in the provinces arrangements had to be co-ordinated with the civic authorities for fire-watching teams available by day and night, and steps were taken to protect the staff and buildings from the effect of air raids. All those who worked in Leadenhall Street will remember long cold hours of anxiety on the roof or in the basement. Henry Tapscott, taking his turn on the roster, showed himself a skilled table tennis player when off duty. In the course of the first year approximately 17 per cent of the staff, mostly under 30, both men and women, were released to join the Forces or for other National Service. This placed extra burdens of office and public duties on those who had to carry on, even though the volume of new business written in all departments dropped away. For those who volunteered or were called-up, the Office, as in 1914–18, undertook to take them back at the end of the war; and for those whose service pay and allowances fell short of £500 a year an allowance to bring them up to this figure was paid. Those who remained found the cost of living inexorably forced up and grants in aid and children's allowances were introduced, but there was no general increase in basic salary levels during those six years of anxiety, with the strains of family anxieties and the trials of rationing and the blackout affecting everyone.

It was thought wise to increase non-profit rates for new business and to halve the Office's life retentions; the latter were further reduced when

78

the full impact of the war was felt under the threat of invasion after the British Expeditionary Force was withdrawn from Dunkirk. Following the practice of FPI in World War I and having regard to civilian casualties from air raids in the Spanish Civil War, war risk cover on new policies was offered to civilians in the UK and Ireland, including those engaged on part-time civil defence duties, but not for those in the services. Under an agreement between the LOA and the Board of Trade life offices agreed to extend the normal period allowed for reinstatement of lapsed policies. In group pension schemes the war risk was at first excluded, but in November 1940 a pool was created for the risk to be shared by the seven leading offices. Friends' Provident took 10 per cent of this pool. The other participants were the Legal & General, Eagle Star, Prudential, each taking 20 per cent, and the North British, Phoenix and Law Union & Rock taking 10 per cent each.

Herbert Rowntree, assistant general manager

The outbreak of war came four months before the end of the Friends' Provident quinquennial term, which was a blow for the actuary, John Robson, who was hoping to recommend his first declaration of a reversionary bonus on a fund which was unusually strong. He felt it right to make exceptionally large reserves to cover depreciation of investments, war-time mortality and expense loadings so that the reversionary bonus declaration had again to be deferred *sine die*, as in 1917, and the interim bonus was held to £1 per cent for the years 1935-39, reduced to 15s 0d per cent from 1st January 1940.

In The Century, which had the proud distinction of paying a reversionary bonus throughout World War I, Willie Robertson, shortly before his untimely death, had to make a similar recommendation, but he was able to keep his interim bonus at £1 per cent for the war years. It soon became clear that other life offices would be forced to adopt a similar policy of caution, but Friends' Provident was to emerge amongst the leaders in its next declaration for the 10-year period 1935-44.

In the investment department the assistant general manager, Charles Bosanquet, resigned to take up a wartime Ministry appointment early in October 1939 and Harold Cope, the joint actuary, took over his responsibilities with Miss Margery Chuter continuing as investment secretary (until her death in 1943), and Miss Millicent Black (Mrs C. Little), as assistant secretary.

The Office responded to the government appeal that life assurance offices should, despite the lower yield obtainable, invest predominantly in Government stock. A large part of the portfolio had been invested in the '30s in industrial and commercial loans. On these, although a few receivers had to be appointed, actual losses were small, and on the large number of mortgages on house purchase terms the losses were very small indeed. Special care, however, had to be taken with the

A Fire Fighting Squad on the roof of 7 Leadenhall Street, 1940

professional loan scheme for doctors, solicitors and accountants, many of whom were absent on service. As income tax was increased from 5s 0d to 8s 6d in the £ the rate of interest on these loans was kept down to 6 per cent gross, to prevent hardship.

It had been a particular pride of Henry Tapscott that during the progressive growth of business after the Depression he had been able to raise the rate of interest on the life fund to over 6 per cent gross and it was a blow to him to see the rate falling to £4 11s 7d per cent over the next four years. One feature which contributed to this was the appeal to boost the War Savings movement by issuing policies payable in War Loan Stock. Notwithstanding the terms of the contract, before the majority of these policies had matured the Office followed the lead of other offices, under pressure from brokers, and paid the proceeds at face value in cash despite the fact that the earmarked stock was standing well below par.

The Century's profitable PHI department brought little new business and a great deal of what was on the books was inevitably lost because of the war-exclusion clause in the policy. The fire department, except for major conflagrations which for the most part were covered by the Government War Damage Scheme, was able to continue to trade profitably with new reinsurance arrangements replacing those made before the war with continental reinsurers. In the accident department there was very little new business to be done in either the motor or the personal accident department, but in other sections trading was profitable. The same applied to the marine department with the underwriting for The Century being handled by the Commercial Union in both London and New York. The Liverpool Marine & General account continued to grow in London and in the Western and Southern States of the USA.

There were two newcomers to the list of subsidiaries of the Century Insurance Trust Ltd in 1939. On the life side the Office took over a small life company called English Estates Assurance Ltd founded in 1921 by Henry Phillips, David Finnie and John Drew. The business of this company was largely confined to non-profit endowment and whole life assurance covering house purchase loans, for the financing of which Friends' Provident had made funds available by way of sub-mortgages. The company was to continue on these lines until the fund was closed in 1968. David Finnie continued until then as chairman of the company.

The second new company was a hire purchase company called Chester & Coles Ltd. The Century had been operating a profitable hire purchase account through its subsidiary The Southern Insurance Company Ltd managed by Harry Hastings and directed by Herbert Rowntree. Chester & Coles Ltd took over this account leaving The Southern to confine its operation to fire and accident insurance in support of The Century in its overseas branches. Before the end of the war the name of Chester & Coles Ltd was changed to Southern Industrial Trust Ltd and that company enjoyed a heyday of prosperity after the war for a further 20 years before it was sold in 1964.

In September 1941 British insurance companies faced the threat of having the assets of their subsidiaries or branch operations in the USA taken over and sold by order of the British government to realise dollars urgently needed for the war effort. The British Insurance Association was able to avoid this by arranging that control of these assets was exercised by the USA government. Adequate reserves had to be held in the USA to cover the branch operation, and remittances to London were restricted to the investment income and only a small proportion of underwriting profits. Any surplus available was paid over to the Federal Reserve Bank of New York for the service of the USA loan to the British government, credit being given to the Office for the amount involved. A resolution of The Century board was required to assign under seal to the British government the aggregate net income of The Century derived in this way from USA business.

Before the end of the war just under half of the pre-war male staff had either volunteered, or had been called up for the services or other duties. Fatal casualties, 15 in number, and prisoners of war each came to about 5 per cent of those on active service. One casualty minuted by the board was happily cancelled when George Swambo, reported killed in an aircraft crashed in the desert, was later reported prisoner, having been sold by an Arab to the enemy.

One great loss for the Office was the death of Hugh Crosfield and his

Willie Robertson, actuary of The Century

wife from a direct hit on their house in Croydon by one of the last V2 rockets which fell in the London area. Hugh Crosfield, who had a family connection with FPI back to 1832, had been a director since 1922 and deputy chairman since 1941.

The Office was very fortunate in the small amount of damage suffered from air raids. Leadenhall Street, where the two main London buildings were situated, was almost unscathed in the bombing in the early part of the war which wreaked such havoc in other parts of the City. In the branches, too, damage was light, except for the destruction of three branch offices at Liverpool, Portsmouth and Hull, and there were no fatal casualties among the civilian staff.

As the war drew to its close the date for the quinquennial valuation for both Friends' Provident and The Century life fund came round again on 31st December 1944. The strong position carried forward in 1939 and the lighter than expected mortality experience during the war enabled John Robson to take the bold decision on his first recommendation for a reversionary bonus five months before the war in Europe ended. As there had been no declaration in 1939 it was the first occasion for a bonus to be declared on the basis of the A1924-29 table of mortality. The reversionary bonus was declared at £1 os od per cent for 1935-39, nil for 1940-42 and £1 5s od for 1943-44. The interim bonus which had been at 15s od per cent during the war was raised to £1 os od per cent.

In the case of The Century the company had taken over in 1943 the sinking fund and PHI business of Friends' Provident and in 1944 ceased to write new life and annuity business. The closed fund was strong and John Robson recommended a reversionary bonus of £1 10s od per cent for the full period of 10 years 1935-44 with an interim bonus at the same rate.

During the war the Office suffered severely by the death of leading personalities. Harold Morland who had been a director since 1914 and chairman of the board since 1928 died in October 1939. He was succeeded by Hugh Seebohm of Barclays Bank Ltd, grandson of Benjamin Seebohm, a founder director of FPI from 1832 to 1871. Early in 1940 Antoine Roques, the office surveyor, died. After long service with The Century and later with Friends' Provident he had made his contribution in the design and construction of three office buildings at Bristol, Manchester and Leeds during the later years of his life. In April 1940 the death occurred suddenly of Willie Robertson, the actuary of The Century since 1908. At the time of his death he was President of the Faculty of Actuaries and the nationally acknowledged authority on permanent health insurance. Over a long period he had been a popular and highly regarded referee in Scotland on Rugby football grounds. After Willie Robertson's death John Robson took over the appointment as

Hugh Seebohm, chairman

actuary of The Century life and PHI funds, with George Meredith as assistant actuary in Edinburgh.

Willie Robertson was the last of the senior officials of The Century from the 1918 period and it was no longer necessary to continue the dual system in London and Edinburgh, except as a formality. All head office functions were therefore moved to London apart from the underwriting, claims and valuation of the PHI department, which for the whole of UK and Ireland continued to be handled in Edinburgh.

This consolidation was confirmed in 1942 by making membership of the boards of FP & CLO and of The Century identical, and changing the board of the Century Insurance Trust in the same way so that joint board meetings of all three could be held. This change was made possible by a revision of the Rules of FP & CLO in that year. The last amendment of the Rules in 1919 had permitted two non-Friend directors only, as representatives of The Century. The new Rule allowed a greater number of non-Friends, provided Friends comprised a majority at all times. Other new rules in 1942 allowed non-Friend local directors overseas, or in specified areas of the UK or Ireland. The voting power of members at a General Meeting was put on a one-member-one-vote basis, with no relation to the size of policies in force, and voting papers for a poll had to be sent only to with-profit policyholders, or to other members who asked for them.

Chapter 6

Moving Ahead in the Post~war Years 1945~57

TWENTY-FIVE YEARS after Henry Tapscott had accepted the appointment as the first general manager of the FPI in the middle of World War I it was again in the strained circumstances of World War II that the selection of his successor had to be made. The whole character of the Office had changed in this time and the demands which would be made on the future chief executive were not easy to define. Under the guidance of the chairman, Hugh Seebohm, it was agreed that the first requirements were the experience, personality and leadership to inspire the branches in a vigorous development programme to handle John Robson's constructive plans for bringing Friends' Provident to the attention of the public and of brokers and agents, and similar plans for The Century under the guidance of Harold Sutcliffe. It had to be faced that, even after 25 years, the name Friends' Provident and Century Life Office was very little known.

Neither in head office nor in the branches was there anyone to meet this challenge and it was not easy to recruit when so many potential leaders in the industry were serving in the forces. Once again the board turned to Edinburgh, and the Scottish directors were asked to make a recommendation. From those considered they selected the assistant manager in Edinburgh of the Guardian Assurance Company, Douglas Pringle, who had wide experience of branch work. He was appointed in January 1942 as deputy manager at Edinburgh head office under Roger Leitch, manager and secretary of The Century. In April 1943 he became deputy general manager of the FP & CLO in London and it was announced that Henry Tapscott, who would be attaining the normal

Aerial view of the Dorking building, taken in 1981 looking West

retirement age of 65 in October of that year, would have his term of office extended to June 1945. It thus covered the date for the announcement of the bonus declaration for the 10-year period 1935–44.

Henry Tapscott in this way happily guided the affairs of the Office right through to the end of the war in Europe, and it fell to Douglas Pringle to set the scene for the next act. After 29 years in the appointment of general manager, Henry Tapscott was elected a director and deputy chairman for a further period of five years. He had brought Friends' Provident from the obscurity of 87 years in Yorkshire as a very small, albeit very successful, denominational life office. From the start in 1916 he had to tackle wartime and post-war difficulties, and then later, after the setback of the Depression in 1929–33, when recovery seemed assured, the stress of World War II had to be faced. It was a great personal achievement that he was able to hand over to Douglas Pringle a strong organisation adaptable and suited for the success which lay ahead for the Office in the next decade. Henry Tapscott was a big man by any standard, and throughout his career he commanded the respect, and earned the deep affection of all who worked with him. His unfailing interest in the Office continuing until his death in 1960 provided a ready source of help for his successors. He kept detailed diaries of events and opinions of people with whom he dealt in the office which present a clear picture of his many interests and projects. Even more detailed diaries, kindly made available by his son, Paul, tell much of his family life. It was a great pleasure also to hear in 1980 from Mrs Marjorie Tapscott, his widow, some of her very clear memories of their days in Bradford in 1916–19 and later in London, and on visits to the States and Canada in the '20s and '30s. He had a rare gift for understanding other people's problems, great and small.

When Douglas Pringle came to London it was soon realised that he had the ability and energy, with a personality of exceptional charm, which were to help him reshape the Home organisation, disrupted by war. His notes of visits to branches show how clearly he picked up their problems before presenting to the directors the report of a Post-war Planning Committee, of which Henry Tapscott made him chairman. Many of the managers and senior officials were absent with the services, and he had limited knowledge of the men from whom he must pick his teams for both head office and the branches. Failure in communication between the underwriting and claims departments at head office and the branches, which had very limited authority, had in the past impaired considerably the service which was being given to the public. Henry Tapscott had realised something of this problem even before the war and had introduced, during the war, an emergency Zone organisation for London branches to improve their relationship with Harpenden. All the

Douglas Pringle, general manager

head office underwriting departments contributed to the report of the Post-war Planning Committee, and Jack Tranter the pre-war fire agency superintendent, with Geoffrey Seabrooke the pre-war Law Courts manager, on his return from army service, advised on the needs of the branches. The outcome was a proposal for decentralisation to seven Zones, or national, chief offices in the UK and Ireland:

North East Zone at Leeds, controlling Bradford, Hull, Newcastle and Sheffield.

North West Zone at Manchester, controlling Liverpool and Kendal.

Midland Zone at Birmingham, controlling Leicester, Northampton and Nottingham.

87

South East Zone at 7 Leadenhall Street, controlling City, West End, Cambridge, Croydon, Ipswich, Norwich, Maidstone, Portsmouth and Romford.

South West Zone at Bristol, controlling Cardiff and Plymouth.

Scotland, where the branches were still on the old Century organisation continued to be controlled from Edinburgh.

Ireland, where the branches at Dublin and Belfast were loosely linked for administrative purposes, but for political reasons, had to communicate independently with Head Office.

The plans mature

The new system not only delegated decisions to the Zone manager and his technical staff but also gave extended authority to individual branches in handling both fire and accident underwriting and claims. This enabled them to meet competition and encouraged the branch staff and Zone officials to give service to meet the proper needs of the client without the restraint of the sometimes over-negative response of the head office underwriters and claims men. The marine underwriter although helpful in his attitude was not prepared to delegate, and it was not until about 35 years later that the actuary conceded that the branches, with the help of a very sophisticated computer system, could be allowed to make any underwriting decision for the life and PHI departments. The Zone organisation did much to facilitate the recruiting, training and retention of both inspectors and technicians needed for the expansion which followed Douglas Pringle's initiative. Internal relationships too were much improved by periodical conferences at both head office and Zone levels. It was a bold new concept which, over the next 15 years, assisted the achievement and control of a rate of expansion far greater than the Post-war Planning Committee could ever have envisaged. The heavy overburden of expenses did in time inevitably force the modification and abandonment of the Zone system but it provided opportunities and training ground for those who would be leading the Office to its place amongst the foremost offices. In its earliest report the committee said that the system called for a 'really live agency manager', but unfortunately this appointment was for a time postponed in order to cut down expenses. It was not until 1950 that the need for an agency manager was conceded when Bill Palmer's appointment did much to break down the 'resistance movement' at head office where, at that time, no member of management other than the general manager had ever worked in a branch. The defences of the 'No'-men were hard to penetrate.

Herbert Tanner,
chairman

As men returned from war service Douglas Pringle had the task of working out a pattern of appointments to fit into head office and the Zone organisation. Several senior branch managers had to be retired to make room for younger men, but most vacancies were satisfactorily filled and the first Zone managers were: South East, Geoffrey Seabrooke; South West, George Palmer; North East, Bill Palmer; North West, Andrew Bryan; and Midland, Dick Cordell; Scotland, Henry Sturrock with George Meredith as assistant actuary; Ireland, Godfrey Goodbody.

The Post-war Planning Committee, under its brief, also dealt thoroughly with accommodation problems and the need for re-training the staff, many of whom had been absent on war service for as much as six years. In-house training courses were arranged, linked with those of the Chartered Insurance Institute, and of the Institute and Faculty of Actuaries. Study in office hours was permitted to help students get through examinations with the aid of accelerated programmes for the syllabuses introduced for diploma courses.

The Committee also reported on the credit scheme introduced by Henry Tapscott and Bernard Brigham in the '30s offering a production bonus to branch managers and inspectors. It was shown to have many shortcomings and failed in its objectives. The scheme was withdrawn and about 12 years later the same fate befell another incentive scheme introduced by Douglas Pringle, which included, on a profit-sharing basis, senior departmental managers and members of management.

It was not long before the Office harvested the first fruits of the seeds of forethought which had been sown by Douglas Pringle and the Post-war Planning Committee. The first full post-war year 1946 gave encouraging promise as to what was to follow later. New life sums assured at £3.9 million were nearly double the pre-war record in 1938, and in 1947 the figure was raised to over £7 million; the PHI department showed a growth of over 25 per cent in the same period. The fire, accident and marine departments results were extremely satisfactory in the UK, but overseas in the USA and Canada anxiety about claims in these departments was revived. In the investment department the yield on the life fund was again raised to £5 4s 0d per cent despite the severe strain of the Government's cheap money policy, which depressed all markets severely by the interest rate of $2\frac{1}{2}$ per cent set for Government stock issued to shareholders in the railway, gas, electricity and mining industries when they were nationalised.

John Robson with the help of the assistant actuary, Dennis Jackson, gave the Office a good lead in the life assurance market with his new schemes based largely on the cover provided by a combination of whole life or endowment policies with family income benefit, and also by stepping up his onslaught on the pensions market.

It was still however an uphill task for the branch staff who found that breaking down resistance to the lengthy and little-known name of Friends' Provident & Century Life Office, with virtually no advertising support, needed a lot more than attractive rates and schemes. It took a further two decades before that obstacle was overcome.

On the general side the name of The Century was more widely known by brokers, and respected by other insurance companies offering re-insurance business. The new Zone organisation did much to improve the service leading to a steady period of premium growth in fire, accident and marine markets. Profits in the home fire department were well maintained but in the accident department difficulties common to the whole market brought major fluctuations in results. The rapid growth of motor insurance soon started the degeneration with which the industry and the car owner became all too familiar. In 1948 the introduction of industrial injuries insurance brought to an end the old Workmen's Compensation Act insurance. Extended common law liability in the

John Robson, actuary

employers' liability and third party sections had to be covered with adaptations to meet the changing influence of court awards and the promotion of claims by trade union officials and solicitors. In certain sections such as personal accident annual contracts, and film producers' indemnity, The Century regained its reputation for initiative, and in the Accident Offices' Association, as in the Fire Offices' Committee, the company maintained its standing alongside the largest groups when mergers reduced the number of independent companies in the London markets over the next 25 years.

The marine department saw difficult times, but in the London market, where The Century was still primarily managed by the Commercial Union – with the subsidiary Liverpool Marine & General also writing both at home and overseas – satisfactory profits were obtained as an offset to losses in the USA which often were heavy.

There were important changes in the board of directors in the war-time and post-war years. Hugh Seebohm who suffered a long illness retired from the chairmanship in 1945, and very shortly afterwards the news of his death was received. He was succeeded by Herbert Tanner, managing director of E. S. & A. Robinson Ltd, of Bristol. In the same year John Little who had joined the staff of The Century as office boy at the time of its formation in 1885 and had been a director of The Century since 1934, and of FP & CLO since 1942, finally retired after 61 years' service. In 1948 Alfred Moorhouse who had entered the service of the Friends' Provident in 1886, and had been actuary from 1904 until 1936, when he joined the board, retired after completing 62 years' service.

The years 1948–57 covered a formative period in which the board called for vigorous expansion by both Friends' Provident and The Century. Douglas Pringle had the backing of a strong chairman in Herbert Tanner and was able to call on the experience of Henry Tapscott as deputy chairman during the years 1945–49 when the proposals of the Post-war Planning Committee were being put into practice. His breadth of vision and enthusiasm gave the stimulus of leadership right through head office and the decentralised Zones. The new organisation worked well from the start, the improved service doing much to build up the status of Friends' Provident, especially in those larger centres where brokers were expanding their share of the life market, and in particular amongst those who were handling pension schemes. Local directors appointed to a board in each Zone helped production staff with introductions and guidance in the campaigns for both life and general business. There was, however, still a reluctance by head office departmental managers to allow full rein to the Zones with a tendency to cling to outmoded systems of duplicate records and counter-checking of decisions. Tension in this respect was not eased until Bill Palmer, who had wide branch and Zone experience, was appointed agency manager in 1950, and later, in 1955, a deputy general manager. This improvement in the relationship between the Zones and head office was carried further by his brother George who followed him in 1955 as an assistant general manager. Maintaining five Zone chief offices, however, with even larger organisations in Edinburgh and Dublin, brought a heavy burden on expense ratios in all departments. Life premium income grew from £1.25 million in 1948 to £6 million in 1957; life sums assured increased steadily over the period except for one small check in 1952. The general insurance premiums of The Century in the UK and Ireland rose from £1.9 million in 1948 to £6.1 million in 1957, but this was not sufficient to keep pace with the rise in expenses. Too often underwriting losses were incurred, especially in the fire, liability and motor departments, and it became clear before the end of this period that modifications in the

Zone system would have to be accepted. This task was tackled by Douglas Pringle's successor.

Douglas Pringle took a keen interest in the growth of The Century branches overseas and although he left their control to Jack Tranter who was appointed deputy general manager in 1955, he made a number of visits to the United States, Canada and Australia where his friendships with local directors, staff and branch connections did much to stimulate the expanding accounts. His main interest, however, was always in the development policy in the United Kingdom and Ireland, for both Friends' Provident and The Century.

The strength of the life fund was demonstrated by the valuation reports prepared by John Robson. The first normal quinquennial valuation was made at the end of 1949. The reversionary bonus was raised from £1 0s 0d per cent to £1 10s 0d per cent, with the interim at £1 5s 0d per cent. The bonus was raised each year during the next quinquennium to £1 17s 6d per cent at the end of 1953. Then in 1954 John Robson surprised the London market by recommending a reversionary bonus of £2 10s 0d per cent, which was not only a record for the Friends' Provident, but was a rate which had hardly ever been equalled by any other British life office at that time; the interim bonus was raised to £2 5s 0d per cent. When he retired a year later, being succeeded by Dennis Jackson FIA, John Robson had seen the aggregate funds of the Office increase from £11½ million to £60 million during his 20 years as actuary. He handed over a strong life fund, with Friends' Provident standing well in the life and pensions markets. On his advice the Century life fund had been closed in 1944, and its reversionary bonus by 1954 had been raised to £5 per cent with a special bonus of £10 per cent for one year. In 1957 the assets of the closed fund, valued and certified by John Andras FIA, were deposited with Friends' Provident at a rate of interest of 6 per cent with a charge for expenses of 10 per cent per annum on the revenue of the fund.

In 1952 the secretary Bernard Brigham, who had joined the Office as accountant shortly before the move from Bradford in 1919, reached retirement age. He had been responsible for the accounting systems of the Office during a long and difficult period, as assistant general manager in 1933 and secretary since 1936. He had introduced early systems of mechanisation including Addressograph, Adrema and Hollerith machines. It was left to his son Michael, who became secretary eight years later on the sudden death of his predecessor, Samuel Mills, to introduce to the Office more modern techniques for cost accounting and the installation of the first computer.

In 1953 Sir Oliver Franks PC, GCMG, KCB, CBE, who had just retired from being British ambassador in Washington, joined the board, and two

Bill Palmer, deputy general manager

years later succeeded his father-in-law Herbert Tanner to become the first non-Quaker chairman. In 1954 he took the chair of a committee of directors formed to guide the management in carrying out the project for the move of the majority of head office to Dorking in Surrey. This far-sighted scheme was the concept of Douglas Pringle, who saw the chance to bring together the main elements of head office which were at the time occupying three different buildings in the City of London, with the accounts department and some other administrative sections still using the war-time hutted accommodation at Harpenden. The office user for the temporary buildings could not be renewed and Douglas Pringle was ahead of his time in seeing in a country office the great advantages in the way of capital expenditure, running expenses, working efficiency and staff health and welfare. The plan was based on concentrating in the country all those departments and sections of head office staff which had no need to be located in the expensive conditions of the City. The Office took a pioneering lead in moving in this way, some five years ahead of the setting-up of the Government's Location of Offices Bureau.

In 1954 part of the Fraser Estate near Dorking (North) Station was bought for £23,000. It comprised 43 acres, mostly in the green belt area of the attractive Mole Valley at the foot of Box Hill, one of the beauty spots of Surrey. It included two mansion houses, Pixham End which was developed for staff sports and social purposes, and Pixham Firs which was sold off. Twenty-five years later it was discovered that the site held some remnants of a Roman villa of the 4th century, including flue and roof tiles, also pottery shards, indicating the importance of the site on the line of Stane Street, the Roman road from Chichester to London. On this site the architects Messrs Easton and Robertson, John Easton and Dr Leslie Preston, designed a building which, at a cost of approximately £450,000, met all the demands for an integrated head office, with room for expansion for the next 20 years, and providing excellent catering, recreational and social facilities. David Tregoning, manager of South West Zone at Bristol, who had been nominated to be deputy general manager and successor to Douglas Pringle, was brought to head office to direct the planning and implementation of the operation. The building was supervised throughout by the premises manager, James Wolfe. Indoor social facilities in Pixham End House included table tennis, a billiards table and a photography dark room. Cricket and association football pitches had as a backcloth the wooded beauty of Box Hill. Tennis courts and a putting course were laid out in the extensive grounds of the estate. Other features included later a licensed bar and facilities for dances, concerts and club meetings, which all contributed to the social life and work of the staff, whose office conditions are very attractive compared with those prevailing in the City, or in other urban

The opening ceremony of the Dorking office. Sir Oliver Franks, chairman, introducing the Lord Mayor of London, Sir Denis Truscott

94

At the opening ceremony, Sir Denis Truscott, Sir Oliver Franks and David Tregoning. On left Douglas and Oliver Pringle and Herbert Tanner

areas. Over the succeeding 25 years additional sports and social facilities have been introduced and run by a strong Sports and Social Club.

So ended in 1957 the Office's 18 years of association with Harpenden, on which many who worked there look back with happy memories. Sympathetic individual consideration was given to those who had to move their homes and there were very few who felt a sense of loss in exchanging the new office conditions and proximity to their homes for the old commuter's life in the City. The opening ceremony of the Dorking building was performed by The Right Honourable the Lord Mayor of London, Sir Denis Truscott TD, on 12th May 1958, with Sir Oliver

96

The original Dorking buildings, opened May 1958

Franks in the chair. Douglas Pringle was there to see his great project realised but he had suffered a severe coronary attack in March 1956, and had been succeeded by David Tregoning at the annual general meeting in 1957. The BBC featured the move on television news but the recorded publicity seems to have been limited. 'Wake up, darling, there's one of my short back and sides' was the reaction of the general manager's hairdresser.

During the '50s the trading results of the general departments of The Century in the UK and Ireland continued a pattern of satisfactory growth in the fire department with profits in most years. In the accident department, however, hazards and claims increased, inadequately matched by premium growth. In many years the resulting losses extinguished profits made in the fire and marine departments. But it was inexorably the trading experience in the fire and motor business in the USA and Canada which dominated the Century profit and loss account, and forced the reduction of the dividend. Between 1951 and 1957 there was only one year in which the USA branch achieved a true underwriting profit, and in the last three years heavy losses were suffered, even after taking credit for interest on the trading reserves. In Canada where the business was controlled by branch managers both fire and motor experience fluctuated considerably but losses were never so serious as those in the United States. In 1957 Jack Tranter, deputy general manager (overseas), made an extensive visit to both countries to lay down severe measures of retrenchment in regard to both underwriting and control of expenses. These had their effect in Canada

Douglas Pringle and the bust which he presented to the Office

where a high proportion of the business written was in the lighter risk area in the Prairies and Western Canada. In the USA, however, the difficulty lay market-wide in the inadequacy of premium rates in all states, and in the deteriorating standards of underwriting and claims settlement which had to be expected from the surviving managing agents. Many of the leaders had either been merged or taken over by major British and American insurance groups, putting them outside the reach of a company as small as The Century. It was already clear that consideration would have to be given as to how long The Century could be allowed to continue to write a preponderant volume of its world-wide fire and motor business in markets which showed no signs of changing their unprofitable trend. It was of no comfort to know that a number of competitors, both British and foreign, were finding themselves in a similar position in their USA branches.

Nevertheless as Douglas Pringle's term of office ended he could look back on a fine record of achievement both at home and overseas. Taking office in the dark days of World War II he had inspired with his drive and

98

At Dorking, should one arrive late, one always gets the guilty impression that the fact does not go entirely unnoticed.

Douglas Young's cartoon – the guilty impression that arriving late at Dorking does not go entirely unnoticed

enthusiasm both head office and all the branches to which he had given the new Zone structure in the UK. Overseas the Australian and Canadian branches of The Century had been given new strength enabling them to provide firm bases for the development of life business for Friends' Provident in Australia and for a new subsidiary Fidelity Life in Canada as described in the next chapter. In Africa too Century branches were established giving an opportunity for the Office's first overseas life venture at Salisbury, Rhodesia in 1954.

Douglas Pringle's greatest legacy was the embryo Dorking scheme which was to bring unmatched advantages to both staff and management in office conditions and efficiency of working, with their effect on welfare and profitability. He had broken new ground to yield a rich harvest for his successors.

Chapter 7

Consolidation and Further Advance 1957-73

WHEN DAVID TREGONING succeeded Douglas Pringle he was the third general manager and the first to be selected from the staff of FP & CLO. He did not have to contend, as his predecessors did, with war-time restraint or post-war planning. He had the support of Dennis Jackson as actuary and a strong management team which included two senior deputy general managers, Bill Palmer (home) and Jack Tranter (overseas), and George Palmer as assistant general manager providing wide experience in both head office and at branches. The Zone organisation was working smoothly and the underwriting departments were settling into the new Dorking office under a team of experienced managers. Overseas too, The Century was faring well except for underwriting losses in USA and Canada. All seemed set in Friends' Provident's 125th Anniversary year to push ahead to reinforce the success achieved in the 12 years after World War II under the leadership of Douglas Pringle. To emphasise the new 'Dorking' era an office emblem was introduced for the Group as a whole, showing the castle which The Century, of Edinburgh, had used for many years, backed by the white rose symbolising the origin of Friends' Provident Institution in Yorkshire.

The overall trading results for 1957, however, brought a series of shocks which made it necessary to review all policy and plans throughout the Group. New business of Friends' Provident and the PHI business of The Century showed progress, albeit offset by worsening expense ratios. The Century's general trading losses however in all departments in the UK, Australia and South Africa were heavy, and the American and Canadian markets produced disastrous results for all

The 'Rose and Castle' emblem used by the Group 1957-73

David Tregoning, general manager and director

Dennis Jackson, actuary

insurers. When at the same time large falls occurred in the Stock Exchange values of quoted investments in both London and New York the Office was cushioned to some extent by having a high proportion of its funds in the UK and Canada invested in mortgages, but the dividend from the large investment in The Century was still a major factor in determining the rate of interest earned on the life fund. Strict instructions were issued for a review of The Century underwriting and curtailment of all expenses throughout the Group. This had its effect generally, but in the USA even after extensive selective pruning of the premium income, and cutting down the New York branch staff by 15 per cent, it was difficult to check rising expense ratios or to improve the profitability of business handled by the managing agents. The question of withdrawing The Century altogether from USA was again considered, as it had been in 1939, but was once more deferred.

In the UK a vigorous retrenchment campaign was carried out under the direction of George Palmer. The main effect of this was to fix the spotlight for the first time on the economic viability of the Zone organisation. The Zones, introduced 11 years earlier, had not, despite their success in other ways, produced premium income adequate to support their overhead expenses. Consideration was given to reducing the number of Zones, but by streamlining procedures, closing minor branches and cutting down the home staff from a total of 1,712 at the beginning of 1958 to 1,556 by the end of 1959, reductions in all expenses were achieved, and, except for merit awards, salaries had to be held at the 1958 level for three years.

Dennis Jackson had taken over a strong position in the life account after John Robson's last record bonus declaration at £2 10s 0d per cent in 1954, but owing to general market conditions in 1957 and 1958 he was not able to recommend an improvement in the interim bonus until the end of 1959, when his first quinquennial valuation raised the reversionary bonus to £2 12s 6d per cent with the interim at £2 10s 0d per cent. Successive years of record new life business, and further records in the pensions and PHI departments had increased recognition of FP & CLO as a name to be reckoned with. At a time when the major composite offices, still engaged with mergers, were concentrating primarily on their general business accounts Friends' Provident's attractive life rates, and the service which the Zones were able to give, brought success particularly in those areas where brokers, both large and small, were increasing their share of the life and pension markets.

During this period of rapidly increasing premium income, the percentage of funds invested in both gilt-edged stocks and unquoted mortgage debentures was reduced and advantage was taken of the improving equity market to seek capital appreciation. Special steps were taken to strengthen the inner reserves and a dividend equalisation account, equivalent to one year's gross dividend at the optimum rate, was set up in The Century to minimise the effect of the violently fluctuating general insurance underwriting results. The Group funds increased from £67 million in 1956 to £168 million in 1964, and the gross rate of interest earned on the life fund was increased from £6 0s 6d per cent to £6 8s 6d per cent.

With appreciation on the quoted investments of over 100 per cent at the end of his second quinquennium Dennis Jackson recommended that the reversionary bonus should be increased to £3 0s 0d per cent with an additional 15s 0d per cent on the bonuses previously attached. The strength of the life fund also enabled him to advise a change from the traditional quinquennial basis for the valuation to a triennial basis. It will be remembered that a resolution to do this in 1932, the centenary year, had to be postponed in the dark days of the Depression and during World War II, but in 1964, when other offices were making a similar change, the actuary could look forward to the advantages of moving into the age of computers.

Roland Gwyn, manager for USA

USA

During the '50s and '60s the underwriting losses of The Century, primarily in USA and to a lesser extent in Canada, never ceased to be a matter of anxiety. The volume of premium income in these two dollar accounts had an overbearing effect on the world-wide fire, accident and marine results, the major source of the Century dividend. It became increasingly clear that to continue in the USA writing so large a premium income through managing agents, a system which gave inadequate branch control, was unlikely to bring the account back to profitability; and indeed, as the records show, 1954 proved to be the last year in which a profit in USA branch was achieved, even after taking into account the interest earnings on the trading reserves. It was therefore at last decided with considerable regret in 1963 to withdraw The Century entirely from USA fire and accident markets in which they had, at times, seen very profitable trading and investment conditions over a period of 60 years. The possibility of taking a share in a pool or a reinsurance syndicate was fully investigated, but there was no satisfactory alternative to complete withdrawal, which meant the retirement of a very loyal branch staff including Roland Gwyn the manager for USA. The marine department continued to write business in New York under the management of the Commercial Union, and in San Francisco through the agency of Rathbone, King and Seeley covering the West Coast states.

Canada

In 1957, the branch and managing agency organisation in Canada was changed, doing away with the Eastern Division in Toronto and bringing the whole of the Dominion under Harry Cutler as manager for Canada in Vancouver, BC.

Although the underwriting losses had been disturbing, the position was nothing like so serious as that in USA as they did not suffer from the difficulties of controlling irresponsible general agents, or from underwriting at rates dictated by politically minded state insurance commissioners. The business was written by brokers and agents supervised by branch managers answerable to the manager for Canada, making it possible to exercise strict control of underwriting and claims settlement. Nevertheless it was necessary to impose close supervision by Harry Cutler in Vancouver of every aspect of the underwriting and branch operation. One of the difficulties encountered was the weakness of discipline in the Canadian Underwriters' Association, the tariff organisation in Canada. In 1963 it was decided to withdraw from this body in all provinces except the Maritimes, gaining a greater freedom for selective underwriting on the smaller risks, especially in Western Canada. By these means the Canadian branches under Harry Cutler were able to maintain, despite some years of adverse underwriting, a further 11 years of satisfactory trading. In 1966 the name of the Pacific Coast Fire, a small Canadian general company taken over in 1920 operating mainly in the western provinces, was changed to The Century Insurance Company of Canada with the required translation of the name in French. All direct writing in Canada was then consolidated in the Canadian company.

Harry Cutler, manager for Canada

Fidelity Life

In July 1957 the decision to enter the life market in Canada, first advocated by John Robson, was implemented by the purchase of 90 per cent of the shares of Fidelity Life Assurance Company of Regina. This small company, founded in 1912, had survived 45 years of very bleak conditions in its home province of Saskatchewan, with some representation in Manitoba, Alberta and British Columbia. Two world wars, the Depression and periods of drought and bad harvest conditions spelt hard times for life assurance in the Prairies before oil was discovered in Alberta. Morley Willoughby the chairman was the son of the company's second chairman, and George Barr QC, the holder of Policy No 1 was still deputy chairman at the age of 79. Under a new general manager, Wynne Eland, the company had moved forward again since

Morley Willoughby,
chairman Fidelity Life

1950 in a period of revival. Acquisition of the company was completed by Dennis Jackson and Harold Cope only shortly before new legislation made it impossible for a Canadian life company to pass into non-Canadian control.

Fidelity Life in its birthplace, Regina, had a very limited potential for development. There was little there to attract to the savage climate of the Prairies the executive and technical staff needed to carry out a policy of expansion. It was decided therefore to move the headquarters in 1960 to Vancouver, BC, where Fidelity could set up a new presence as a leading life company in Western Canada, joining The Century and Pacific Coast Fire which were already prominent in the West in the general insurance field. Fidelity Life Building at 1112 West Pender, Vancouver, was erected for their joint headquarters and all the companies, directed by one strong Canadian board, had the advantage of sharing overhead expenses. Wynne Eland retired in 1961, handing over to Murray Marven, by which time a policy of expansion supported by new products was established, but restraint had to be set for Fidelity to develop within its own financial resources, without relying on remittances from London.

Australia

The possibility of entering the life field in Australia was first raised in 1957 by the Australian directors of The Century at a time when the large mutual life companies, which dominated the Australian market, were

*Fidelity Life
(Saskatchewan Life)
Policy No 1 21st May
1914, issued to George
Barr QC (ABOVE) who
was vice president of the
company when he died in
1960 aged 82*

starting to compete in the general insurance field by taking over some of the smaller portfolios, or by the formation of subsidiary companies. Following the analogy of the acquisition of the Fidelity in Canada, an approach from the Australian Metropolitan Life was investigated, but terms with this company could not be agreed. There was no other chance at that time to take over an Australian life company, so it was decided to take the bold step of setting up in 1960 an overseas branch organisation of Friends' Provident, writing a separate series of policies under Australian statutory control, with its chief office at Sydney, NSW. Dennis Jackson was actuary to the new fund and management and board supervision was retained in London, but to compete in the Australian market the branch had to be a fully fledged Australian operation. The recruitment in Australia of staff for the chief office was not easy. Craig Grainger, The Century manager, did not have the qualifications required to manage an independent life fund, so Alan Wylie, FIA, from the Australian Mutual Provident was appointed general manager for Australia. Phil Burns, FIA, a member of the Dorking actuarial staff was selected to be life manager and assistant actuary, and John Nott, manager of Bristol branch, was sent out in 1961 to supervise administration and the underwriting of The Century branches. The strong local board of The Century helped greatly, especially in the early years. There were, however, serious growing pains in setting up the new organisation, particularly in recruiting an agency force for the direct selling system in competition with the well-entrenched members of the Australian Life Offices' Association, in which the mutual life offices held the lead. Control from Canberra was strict and in 1965 it was necessary to appoint a stronger manager for Australia. Robin Gray, assistant general manager (overseas) was sent out to take over, and did a good job putting new strength into both Friends' Provident and The Century in Australia.

UK Branch Organisation

In the UK the retrenchment campaign in 1958–59 had done much to reduce expense ratios, and life new business continued to grow steadily, but heavy losses in the fire, accident and motor departments led in 1964 to a complete review of the Zone organisation. Much had been achieved in the service given to the public by decentralisation, but the premium income growth was not sufficient to match increased overhead expenses at a time when competition in all departments was getting more keen. Provided the branches were using their underwriting and claims authority properly routine work could be done more economically and efficiently at Dorking; and producers, given support by more technical staff, could be relieved of much of their administrative work. Major underwriting and claims questions could also be strictly controlled by departmental managers at Dorking.

In the place of the five English Zones three administrative Regions were organised: Southern Region, comprising all the branches in the South East and South West Zones, was controlled from Dorking by the assistant general manager (home), Bill Bailey; the Midland Region which took over South Wales was managed by Graham Pollard at Birmingham; and all the North East and North West Zone branches came into the Northern Region at Leeds under Jim Smith-Goode.

The organisation in Scotland and Ireland was left unchanged. The committee which worked out the changes involved was under the chairmanship of George Palmer, deputy general manager, shortly before

Sir Denzil Macarthur-Onslow, CBE, DSO, ED, chairman Australian Advisory Board

George Palmer, deputy general manager

Lord Franks, chairman

he retired in January 1965. He was assisted by Dewi Lloyd Humphreys and Bill Bailey who had been appointed assistant general managers in 1961. It was a definite swing back to centralisation, but it did not curtail the authority of producers in the field, and it brought into head office the ingredients for the early computer programmes which were being prepared. Consideration was given by management to the setting up of some life-only branches, but on the grounds of the cost to Friends' Provident of doing so, and the loss of some of the advantages of mutual support, it was decided to continue the composite operation which had given strength to FP & CLO since 1918.

Southern Industrial Trust Ltd

During the early '60s thought had to be given to the policy for the development of the hire purchase business of The Century, which had been handled in the subsidiary Southern Industrial Trust Ltd for over 20 years, with its accounts consolidated in The Century Group. A change in the tax ruling on inter-company loan interest made it necessary to seek other forms of financing development in an industry which was expanding rapidly in a climate of keen competition. The Century invested a further £250,000 in the ordinary shares of SIT and bank loans were arranged, but, to keep pace with the market, finance injection would have exceeded the amount which could rightly be taken from the resources of a mutual life assurance office of the size of Friends' Provident at that time.

The company had continued to trade profitably under its managing directors, Robert Trinder, followed by Edward Heath, but by 1963 SIT faced the added difficulty of recruiting senior specialist staff for a company too small to compete profitably with the subsidiaries of major clearing banks, which were taking over a large proportion of the market. It was decided to seek a merger and an approach was welcomed in 1962 from The Wagon Finance Corporation Ltd of Sheffield to purchase the shares of SIT with full protection for the staff of the company. Negotiations were delayed for a while but by the end of 1963 the deal was completed. In addition to a substantial cash sum paid for the shares the Office secured a 10 per cent interest in Wagon Finance, with David Tregoning representing the Office on their board. Forty years of profitable dealing in hire purchase finance ended with a satisfactory investment and a good capital profit. SIT executives succeeded to important posts in the Wagon Group, including board appointments for Henry Hicks and Fred Prain.

Board and Management

By the early '60s much had been achieved by the management team carrying on the vigorous post-war policy of development for both Friends' Provident and The Century. The Office had earned recognition not only by its share of the life and pensions business underwritten, but also by its contribution to the committee work of the industry in the Institute of Actuaries and the Life Offices' Association, and in the affiliated bodies of the British Insurance Association. In the Chartered Insurance Institute David Tregoning held office as president in the Jubilee year 1961–62, and as a member of Council took a leading part in its careers work. A number of branch managers were presidents of their local institutes, and served on CII committees and the Council.

There were changes on the Board. Sir Oliver Franks (later Lord Franks), when appointed Provost of Worcester College, Oxford, handed over the

AGM at Dorking, May 1963, from left M. Brigham, M. Rowntree, M. Cadbury, E. Phillips, Lord Ferrier, R. Wotherspoon, A. Braithwaite, Lord Seebohm, D. Marshall, P. Priestman, J. Fox, L. Gray, D. Tregoning and H. Douglas

chairmanship in 1962 to Frederic Seebohm, son of Hugh Seebohm, who had been chairman in the war years 1939–45, and a great-grandson of Benjamin Seebohm, a founder director of FPI 1832–70. In the following year the retirement of Philip Priestman brought to an end the long association with the Priestmans of Bradford and Hull, 1832–1919 without a break, and 1948–63, including three outstanding chairmen, John 1856–66, Frederick 1886–1908 and Henry B. 1908–17.

Changes in the management included the retirement in 1959 of Bill Palmer, who had given infectious drive and initiative to the UK and Ireland branches as agency manager in 1950 and deputy general manager in 1954. Following him as deputy general manager his brother George brought leadership and guidance not only to the branches but also to the head office managers responsible for underwriting policy and procedure. He took a leading part in the modernising of administration and management accounting systems introduced in the '60s. When he retired in 1965 Dennis Jackson, the actuary, was appointed deputy general manager and actuary.

On the overseas side Jack Tranter retired in 1961 after 50 years with the Group. The last of the senior executives who were Century men in 1918, he had managed the profitable home fire department between the wars before assuming responsibility for all the general developments overseas from 1948 to 1961 in a period of rapid branch expansion in the USA, Canada, Australia, New Zealand, Denmark and throughout South, Central and East Africa, with agencies in many other territories. He was succeeded by Robin Gray as assistant general manager and subsequently by Brian Stone when Gray went to Australia in 1965.

Harold Cope, chief assistant general manager, had been responsible for the investment of the funds of Friends' Provident and its subsidiaries for 22 years, not only in the UK but in all the overseas territories since 1943, with the mortgage and professional loan side managed by Peter Leishman. Despite the tough conditions during World War II, and the even greater strain of the post-war era, rapid expansion increased the funds of the Group from £16.1 million to £168.1 million during his time, and the gross interest rate on the life fund was raised from a low point at £4 9s 5d per cent in 1940 to £6 8s 6d per cent in 1964. Loan finance was used extensively to support The Century premium growth and building societies were developed in Rhodesia, Zambia, Nigeria and Jamaica. To succeed him in 1965 Reginald Harding was appointed assistant general manager.

Harold Cope, chief assistant general manager

1965–73

The next decade was to be one of great advance and change for the Office both at home and overseas. In 1968 Frederic Seebohm (later Lord Seebohm) gave up the chairmanship on account of his other commitments but remained on the board. Edwin Phillips, MBE, one of the managing directors of Lazard Brothers, merchant bankers with whom the Office had had close associations for more than 50 years, became the first chairman who had no personal connection with the Society of Friends. Later in the same year David Tregoning, the first general manager to be appointed from the staff, became also the first executive director of FP & CLO. The old tradition in the industry that the boards of insurance offices should be entirely non-executive was changing at that time. An announcement was made in 1969 that David Tregoning would be retiring at the end of 1971 and would be succeeded by Dewi Lloyd Humphreys, who was appointed deputy general manager, but tragically,

Lord Seebohm, chairman

in June 1970, a drowning accident in British Columbia deprived the Office of this executive officer's wide experience and outstanding qualities. Bill Stubbs, formerly assistant manager for Canada of The Century and general manager for Australia since 1968, was transferred to London to be chief assistant general manager as soon as his successor in Sydney, Jack Lamb, had taken over from him. He was subsequently appointed deputy general manager, and at the AGM in 1973 succeeded to David Tregoning, whose retirement had been postponed for 17 months.

Later in 1970 the Office suffered another severe loss by the death of Reginald Harding, aged 46, assistant general manager (investments) since 1965. He was succeeded by Michael Hardie. Sadly too, Dennis Jackson, who had retired as deputy general manager and actuary at the end of 1971, died only six months later. As actuary from 1956 he had played a great part in extending the ideas of John Robson in the life and pensions department in the period of rapid expansion after World War II.

He was also responsible for launching the Friends' Provident branch in Australia and seeing it through its difficulties in the first 10 years. In his time the Office established its claim to rank amongst the first 12 British life offices in terms of new business reported each year. The Group funds which had doubled over the quinquennium 1960–64, standing then at £114 million, had been more than quadrupled by the end of 1974. The credit for this was shared by Dennis Jackson and the deputy actuary, Doug King, who designed attractive new schemes to meet the changing needs of policyholders affected by fiscal measures, such as capital gains tax and estate duty, and by the remorseless shocks of inflation and rising interest rates. The demand for an equity linked policy led to the formation of Friends' Provident Unit Trust Managers Ltd in 1969, as the investment factor assumed greater importance in both the short and long-term policies. The UK reversionary bonus rose from £3 per cent (plus 15 per cent of attached bonuses) in 1964 to £4 per cent at the end of 1970. The proportion of with-profit business written rose steadily as Friends' Provident was established firmly in the brokers' market.

Dewi Lloyd Humphreys, deputy general manager

The volume of business written in the Republic of Ireland grew rapidly, leading to the introduction of a separate Irish series of with-profit policies, reflecting the investment conditions in the Republic, so that when, in 1969, a terminal bonus of 20 per cent on attached bonuses was introduced for the main UK series this did not apply to the new Irish series until an adequate rate of interest was earned on the Irish investment portfolio. The UK terminal bonus was raised in 1972 to 25 per cent and has been adjusted periodically both up and down in ensuing years following major changes in market values.

The reputation of Friends' Provident as a pensions office continued to grow, particularly amongst insurance brokers. The proportion of the total premium income written in the pensions department in the UK and Ireland rose to over 40 per cent in the late '60s and to 48 per cent in 1974. Behind these figures lay a tremendous amount of work handled by the department under the direction of Doug King. The complete review of schemes led to changes in their form, and gave individual pensioners the advantage of with-profit annuities. There followed several years during which the Office had to keep pace with repeated changes by successive governments in the proposals for state pension schemes, with no certainty as to how the Office schemes could be linked to any one of them, until 1975 when the Labour Government Social Security Pension Scheme was at last carried through. This involved the overhaul of all schemes for employers who used them as a basis for contracting out of the Government scheme. In the pensions market throughout this time the excellent and steadily improved bonuses on the with-profit business did much to make the Office's terms attractive.

Reginald Harding, assistant general manager, investments. President, Society of Investment Analysts

Doug King, general manager and director, actuary

In 1967 English Estates Assurance Ltd, which had been a wholly owned subsidiary since 1939, was closed for new business in keeping with the policy of reducing the Office's investment in house purchase loan business which had been almost the sole source of business for English Estates for 30 years. This meant the retirement of David Finnie, a very good friend of the Office, who had been chairman of the company since its foundation in 1921 as an independent company.

In The Century the closed life fund continued to be run down but the bonus declaration was changed to a triennial basis in 1967 to conform with the requirements of the Companies Act of that year. By 1974 the reversionary bonus was standing at £5 per cent per annum plus a special bonus of £6 per cent at the end of each triennium, with an interim bonus rate of £5 per cent. Ignoring a very small sinking fund account the long term activity was in the strong PHI department. Keeping to the tradition since its origin in 1885 the PHI account was managed from Edinburgh with George Meredith as the assistant actuary from 1955–64 followed by Donald Biggs who retired in 1971 and was succeeded by Frank Martin. The Century lead in this market was maintained despite the attack by several new competitors attracted by the success of The Century. The rapid growth in the gross premium income from £500,000 in 1964 to over £1 million in 1971 and £1.5 million in 1974 was given stimulus by developing for the benefit of industrial and commercial employers the group schemes originally introduced for the benefit of professional associations and similar groups.

Australia

In the period of 1965–67 during which Robin Gray was the general manager for Australia he did a great deal to strengthen the management team, particularly in the very volatile area of the agency force which is the basis of the direct selling operation of the Australian mutual life offices. He also introduced improved procedures for the administration of the branches and the relationship between the Australian management and London. The newly defined Australian Advisory Board gave very valuable guidance under the chairmanship of Sir Denzil Macarthur-Onslow, succeeded by Lawford Richardson, both of whom had served the Group well since the setting up of The Century Australian branch in 1951. For family reasons Robin Gray asked to be relieved, and in 1968 he was transferred to Vancouver where Harry Cutler, the manager for Canada of The Century, was to retire in 1969. In his place Bill Stubbs, assistant manager for Canada, took over in Sydney and brought fresh vigour to the Australian life and general branches until he joined the London management. At the end of 1970 Jack Lamb, recruited from the Northern Assurance Company, became general manager for Australia.

In 10 years the Australian life account, despite growing pains, had gained stability and made progress. Expenses were controlled and the bonus earned was, by Australian standards, satisfactory. The decision to set up and finance from London an independent branch under Australian regulations had proved its worth to the main fund.

Canada

The two Canadian subsidiaries, Fidelity Life and Pacific Coast Fire (The Century of Canada after 1966), following the move of Fidelity to Vancouver in 1960, had the same chairmen, Frank Brown, CBE, followed by Reg Miller, but not identical boards, as long as the link with Regina for Fidelity was preserved. In 1968 the chair was taken over by

Hon Wm Hamilton, PC, OC, an outstanding personality who had been Conservative Postmaster-General in the Dominion parliament, and the opportunity was taken to reduce the total number of directors with the same members on both boards. At the same time the administrative services of the two companies were centralised, making a considerable saving of costs which were tending to run high. Improvement in trading results and administration were achieved after a visit to Canada shortly after his retirement in 1965 by George Palmer.

Robin Gray retired in 1971 and Gordon Elliott succeeded as president of The Century of Canada. In the same year Murray Marven, general manager of Fidelity, retired and Alan Broadbent, a very senior executive recently retired from a major Canadian company, was brought in to hold office as president and chief executive officer of Fidelity until the actuary, Stewart Cunningham, took over this appointment in 1973. This, with other new appointments, brought new motivation to the company under a strong Canadian board, so it was agreed that there should be some relaxation in the restraint which had required them to plan their development without calling on Friends' Provident for additional finance.

UK and Ireland

Just 10 years after the formal opening of Dorking head office, the management committee under Dewi Lloyd Humphreys had reported in 1968 on difficulties of recruiting in the Dorking area and also overcrowding in the office. where the two originally planned extensions had already brought the building to the limits set by the planning authority. After various alternatives had been considered the management once again in 1969 turned to Edinburgh, where staff could be found, and space for a new centre was made by enlarging the Charlotte Square property, and later by acquiring a large club building nearby. This centre included the head office PHI department and handled the majority of routine work in both life and general departments for Scotland and for the Northern and Midland branches in England. In these areas the work for the branches handled by Edinburgh grew to something like 35 per cent of the total UK operation. The centre was also able to relieve Dorking by taking over, at a time of high pressure, an important section of the pensions department work together with the related accounts and renewals.

The work load of the centre was increased over the next 5 years, and in 1974 pressure of space once again forced a move to leasehold premises in a newly erected office block at 31 St Andrew Square. This building gave all that was required, but those who appreciated the quiet dignity of the

18th century building in Charlotte Square, which had been the home of The Century for just 70 years, may be excused for regretting the move. The turn of events however was to bring an end to the Edinburgh centre in 1975, when space became available at Dorking. The decision was made to concentrate there all departments or sections of head office from Edinburgh, London and Worthing which would be linked with the major plans for the fully integrated operation of the computer. The centre had been developed as an efficient and well managed unit and its closure brought change for individuals and some disruption of family life. This, with a few inevitable redundancies, led to an unfortunate head-on clash with the union, ASTMS, and an unsuccessful challenge to the board at the AGM in London in 1976.

Hon Wm Hamilton, OC, chairman Fidelity Life

The management committee supported by the line managers continued to study a wide range of forward planning issues. In 1971 the branch organisation in the UK was closely examined and it was agreed that, even accepting some increase in expenses, it was no longer advantageous for the life business of Friends' Provident, with the PHI Department on the one hand, or for the short-term business of The Century on the other, to be handled together in composite branch offices. Long-term branches could operate larger areas with a small staff, whereas for The Century a smaller number of larger branches with more technical staff could offer a better service to the public, each side concentrating on its particular planning objectives. Outside and inside staff could be trained as specialists in their own skills, rather than in the role of 'Jacks of all trades' as the complexity of the business kept growing. The standards of productivity and staff career prospects could be enhanced and new and improved systems of cost accounting, applied separately to life and general departments, would give a better measure of accountability for the branch performance and the allocation of administration overheads.

The outcome in 1972 was the establishment of 20 Friends' Provident branches in the UK and Ireland and 20 Century branches for the UK alone. This entailed a number of changes amongst the managers and senior staff but the moves worked out smoothly, and were well accepted. In Ireland no further change was needed because since 1971, on account of the heavy losses in the fire and accident departments, the Irish branches had been writing only life, pensions and PHI business. The Century portfolio of general business had been taken over by the Shield Insurance Company, an Irish associate of the Eagle Star Group. Following the splitting of the branches in this way the name of the parent office was changed to Friends' Provident Life Office with the general insurance branches continuing under the name of The Century both in the UK and overseas. A new office emblem for the Group embodying the

*Michael Brigham,
assistant general manager*

letters FP & C in modern style was adopted in 1973 in place of the Rose and Castle emblem which had been used since 1957.

The Group funds increased from £168 million to £380 million in the '70s and with the life, pensions and annuity premium income growing at a rate of 15 to 20 per cent per annum, the management of the office's investments first by Reginald Harding, and later by Michael Hardie, was a very important back-up feature of the corporate planning. The withdrawal of The Century from USA in 1963, followed by the selling of the domesticated Century of New York, had left the Office with a US dollar portfolio having a market value of £9.7 million in excess of trading liabilities, but elsewhere assets and liabilities were generally kept in balance. Where possible in Africa withdrawal of funds followed the closing down of trading, but in Rhodesia approximately £3 million surplus to liability was locked in by the local regulations resulting from the Unilateral Declaration of Independence in November 1965. In Australia new legislation, later relaxed, required transfers from the main life fund to the statutory fund there, and investment of this fund was subject to direction by the Australian government. Over the decade the gross rate of interest on the main fund improved from 6.42 per cent to 7.59 per cent. Already, however, inflation, rising interest rates, statutory control of wages and dividends, and a crisis amongst smaller finance houses were throwing shadows of world-wide problems still to come.

David Tregoning was fortunate to have a strong line-management team during these years when much was done in the improvement of administration in the area of Organisation and Methods and management accounting. Budgeting systems and reports were introduced and a start was made on tailoring clerical and statistical work in such a way that it could be made to fit into a future computerisation programme. These improvements, coupled with the increase in life new business, helped to hold down unit costs. In consultation with Hay MSL considerable attention was given to a comprehensive review to form a foundation for a modern salary and administration system, which introduced rates based on job evaluation and merit awards, subject to annual appraisal. In 1971 the committee of the internal Staff Association which had helped management with staff problems for 25 years advised their members to seek union representation, and recognition for union members was negotiated with the Association of Scientific Technical and Managerial Staffs (Union of Insurance Staffs section), which had taken over the former Guild of Insurance Officials. Soon after this a Line Managers' Association was recognised to represent more senior members of the staff.

The very rapid growth of business in all departments in the UK and Ireland during the '60s focused attention on the urgent need for studying

Diagram of the first Honeywell computer installation

the potential for further mechanisation, including possible use of computers which had been extensively developed in the USA and were being progressively introduced by leading British offices. A computer committee under the chairmanship of Michael Brigham was charged with the study of any operation which could be transferred to a computer, and the type of computer which would best meet the Office's needs. Prominent amongst those who worked on this committee were William Rowlandson, Ted Whiting, Allen Cullum and Frank Ward. A visit to America by Michael Brigham and William Rowlandson led to the purchase of a Honeywell '400' computer on special terms because it was their first computer sold to a British insurance company. With Honeywell's help a team of programmers and operators was built up from members of the life, pensions and accounts departments, with Ted Whiting as manager, assisted by Brian Nunn and William Rowlandson. Simple programmes were written for pensions renewals, but it was primarily in the fire, accident and administration departments that the best results were first achieved. There was good liaison between the computer team and the user departments through the management Computer Steering Committee and as the work grew a second generation Honeywell '1200' and another '400' were installed. When the American consultants, McKinsey & Co, were asked in 1966 to advise on the whole administration of the Office, and on the computer department in particular, it was gratifying that they spoke well of both the planning and achievements of this in-house team.

In 1965 Michael Brigham was appointed assistant general manager in charge of mechanisation, handing over the secretaryship to Raymond Johnson. A great deal of research by his team involved the study of

Rugby Football Team, 1975 winners of the Preece Cup

different systems and possible expansion of the Office's computer operation. One programme, devised at Dorking, was actually sold to another life office. They always had as a long term objective the introduction of a fully integrated scheme to handle all aspects of the long term business, but with the limitations of the computer carrying the load of the Century general programme this was not yet possible. In the greatly changed circumstances 10 years later their dream was to come true with dramatic effect on the structure and operation of the office in the UK and Ireland. Before that however Michael Brigham had resigned making way for the new leadership which was to take the Office far into new territory in the computer world. Much had been achieved but new horizons were coming into sight.

At the AGM in 1973 David Tregoning retired as general manager, continuing as a director until 1979. In his time the growth of the Office, following on the post-war planning of Douglas Pringle, gathered momentum as appears in the statistics in Appendix IV. From 1956 to 1972 new life sums assured had increased tenfold and the life assurance fund sixfold. In the UK and Ireland the decentralised zone and branch organisation was rationalised, giving better control from head office and better service to the public and policyholders. By 1972 separate branches for Friends' Provident and for The Century had been established, to concentrate maximum potential effort on each side of the organisation.

New management accounting systems, evolved by the secretarial and accounts departments, provided the tools to develop corporate plans and to check performance at all levels. Improved recruitment and training facilities raised the standard and performance of managers and staff, especially those of the professionally qualified executives at head office and the production staff in the field. Much of this came directly from the success of the Dorking scheme, the fruits of which were seen in measurable quantum in the way of reduced expenses and improved efficiency, and also in the morale, health and welfare of those who worked there. These advantages are cumulative as each new development is made easier by the facilities and atmosphere which Dorking offers.

Overseas, David Tregoning was able to develop the close links, based on warm friendship, which his predecessors enjoyed with both directors and staff. In Canada the purchase of Fidelity Life in 1957 was the first independent overseas life venture, and in Australia the Friends' Provident life branch, started in 1960, was brought through to maturity. In Africa on the other hand promising developments in South Africa, the Rhodesian Federation, East Africa and Nigeria, built up for both Friends' Provident and The Century, were swept away in the flood of nationalism which drove many British insurers out of the continent.

It is probably fair to say that the change in this period which marked most clearly the improved status of the Office was the general recognition accorded to the name Friends' Provident in UK and Ireland, and in Australia, as one of the leading mutual life offices. With virtually no advertising in any form it had been a long uphill road towards this objective for those who had to sell the name before and after World War II. Looking forward and using the slogan 'Friends for Life', the Office had a firm base for future planning and publicity.

Chapter 8

Parting with The Century and the Relaunch 1973-80

BILL STUBBS WAS appointed to succeed David Tregoning as general manager at the AGM in 1973 with a seat on the main boards. After long experience in Canada with the Sun Alliance group he had joined The Century as assistant manager for Canada 1964–68, before an unexpected vacancy led to his appointment as general manager for Australia for two years. He then came to London in 1970. At each stage he had shown outstanding ability and a very quick grasp of the affairs of the Office, in Canada, Australia and New Zealand. He was the first senior executive to come to London having intimate knowledge of the managers and the problems of staff in those countries. He also had experience of the Canadian and Australian agency systems of life assurance marketing which were growing rapidly in importance for the Office. He soon established his position in head office and branches in the UK where his style of leadership and ready encouragement of talent and new ideas were quickly recognised and accepted. He was well supported by his closest colleagues Fred Cotton, deputy general manager, and Doug King, the chief assistant general manager and actuary. With the assistant general managers it was a team very well qualified to plan and carry out the programme of development being worked out for both Friends' Provident and The Century. There was strength in the departments throughout the organisation, but for The Century the shadow of change was already appearing in 1973.

By 1974 the life and general branches, separated in 1972, were beginning to show advantages of specialisation by way of proper costing and better control of expenses. A new Life Marketing Organisation

Bill Stubbs, chief general manager and director

123

under Michael Doerr an assistant general manager at head office, assisted by Malcolm Payne in the field, was formed to develop all aspects of marketing long-term products and to re-train the staff in their specialist techniques. New advertising material enlivened sales campaigns, and new incentive bonuses, and competitions for branch and individual performance encouraged productivity. The LMO provided close links between the field staff and the strong team of actuaries and agency officials at head office. In addition to raising the standards of service to policyholders and brokers it did much to improve morale in the branches.

In The Century more complex issues were encountered in the growing difficulties of economic strain in 1973 and 1974. The fire department losses, including weather claims, were heavy and underwriters had to adjust to the Fire Offices' Committee reduction in tariffs after a reference of the FOC to the Monopolies Commission. In the accident and marine departments perennial difficulties of underwriting and claims persisted, and the struggle to match the expense ratios of large competitors continued. In these circumstances it was not easy to meet branch or individual targets in the home branches. Overseas the Canadian and Australian general insurance markets were again simultaneously in distress, which hit The Century particularly hard as more than a quarter of its world-wide fire account was in these two countries.

As the year 1974 progressed it had to be faced that events were building up to a situation which held for the Office a change as dramatic, and much more traumatic, than those which had altered the course and very nature of Friends' Provident in 1915 and 1918. It was to mean the parting with The Century and all its subsidiaries.

There had been anxiety growing over several years that some strengthening of the capital and reserves of The Century would become necessary if the solvency margin of assets over liabilities of the company was to be increased adequately for a developing general account, although The Century had kept its margin at more than twice the 10 per cent statutory requirement. In 1973 the nominal and issued capital was increased by one million ordinary shares which were taken up by Friends' Provident on terms which injected £2.5 million new capital, leaving a similar amount uncalled. It was reckoned that by using retained profits and investment capital gains the situation could then be held for several years. There were however changes ahead which, coming in a period of unusually heavy losses both at home and overseas, produced insurmountable difficulties. First, the general deterioration in the British economy led to a spiralling rate of inflation which seriously threatened the company's position. Mounting expenses, depreciated investments and the strain of achieving real growth were combined with poor prospects for profits from trading. Secondly, new regulations announced by the Department of Trade mid-year were even more stringent than anticipated. The requirements for the separation, admissibility and valuation of assets meant a large reduction in the solvency margin. It was also known that EEC regulations would shortly require the statutory asset margin to be increased considerably.

Other important regulations applied to any mutual life office which held more than one-third of the share capital of a general insurance company; and Friends' Provident was, of course, one of the very few life offices in this position. The value of a general subsidiary to a mutual life office could only be calculated in relation to its free assets. The effect of this 'look through' requirement was to reduce the value of The Century to less than half the written down book value in the Friends' Provident balance sheet. Injection of further capital by the Office to top up The Century's solvency margin would, in effect, be lost. With poor dividends in prospect the inevitable effect on the life fund was unacceptable. Alternative sources of capital for The Century were explored but offered no likelihood of success. The board and management were forced very reluctantly to accept that they could not feel confident of the viability of The Century in the Group. A most important consideration was that there could be no certainty that Friends' Provident could continue to offer The Century staff, either at home or overseas, satisfactory career prospects in a company denied development prospects by enforced financial stringency and the expectation of further government restraint.

It was not until well into the year 1974 that it was possible to get a clear view of the economic outlook or of the new regulations which were to come into force on 1st January 1975, so time was limited. The board and management had the agonising task of finding the best long-term course for the benefit of Friends' Provident policyholders both at home and in Australia, while at the same time giving all possible consideration to the interests of the staff world-wide of both The Century and Friends' Provident. Naturally every possibility of keeping The Century in the Group was explored, but there was no alternative to the sad conclusion that this could not be done. Even if it had been possible to make a pooling or reinsurance arrangement this would have eclipsed the future for The Century staff.

The size and character of every British company which would absorb The Century with the minimum of friction was very carefully studied. An opportunity to approach the Phoenix, an office with which The Century had enjoyed good relations over many years, brought a most welcome response. Negotiations conducted by Bill Stubbs and his colleagues in a

Alfred Braithwaite,
deputy chairman

very friendly atmosphere, and with praiseworthy security, were concluded in November. It was agreed that on 1st January 1975 The Phoenix would take over The Century Insurance Company Ltd and all its subsidiaries and interests world-wide in exchange for a substantial holding of the shares of the enlarged Phoenix Group. By a temporary reinsurance arrangement, and a subsequent agreement, the long term funds of The Century remained with Friends' Provident. They comprised the closed Century life fund, the PHI fund and the small sinking fund account. Once it was accepted that the parting was unavoidable it was a relief to know that The Century staff would be joining a company of similar outlook and philosophy, and one which would be an unlikely target for a further take-over bid having regard for the large shareholdings of Friends' Provident and The Continental Group of New York.

The chairman, Ted Phillips, was invited to join the Phoenix board, and

126

Bill Stubbs retained his directorship of The Century. Brian Stone, an assistant general manager of the Group, was promoted to be general manager and a director of The Century with a special care for the implementation of all aspects of the changeover. He subsequently held an important appointment for the Phoenix Continental at Brussels. The Phoenix made it clear from the start that they would offer full career prospects to qualified members of the Century staff as they were at that time actively seeking more technical strength. Other names which appeared on Phoenix doors at their head office in the City included those of Richard Blackman the marine underwriter and Ken Fenn the foreign accident manager.

By any standard the ending of long and happy associations covering 57 years, and involving the separation of close personal friends, was a change which no-one could accept without deep feeling. It was particularly hard that it had to be accepted under outside pressure and at a time when The Century home branches and departments were proving their strength in the separate branch organisation introduced in 1972. In Australia the short term branches of the two companies merged and in Canada the Century of Canada continued to function as a Western Canada base for the Phoenix Group. In Rhodesia the Phoenix branch joined The Century subsidiary. The chief officers and the directors in each country were confidentially informed of the progress of negotiations but even so the unexpected announcement was a particular shock to those at a distance who had served The Century well over many years.

Friends' Provident Life Office Act 1975

In 1972 the board had given consideration to up-dating the Rules of the Office which had last been amended in 1942. This provided an opportunity to reconsider the requirement that a majority of the board of directors had to be members of the Society of Friends. The Quakers felt strongly that in view of the name and origin of the Office they should be able to influence decisions on practice or policy which affected their religious principles. The board and management were unanimous in not wishing to abandon the sentimental link with the Society of Friends, but it had to be admitted that there would be increasing difficulty in finding amongst Friends' directors having the right experience and stature to contribute to the growing volume and complexity of the business of the Office. There was already a proposal that additional executive directors, unlikely to be Friends, should be elected to the board and their election might be barred if the 1942 Rule was not changed. It was therefore agreed that instead of the Quaker majority required by the 1942 Rules there should be at least 5 Friends in a board membership of not more than 20 and not less than 10 directors. For this minority a power of decision was to be reserved on matters which, in their unanimous opinion, raised issues involving Friends' principles. A majority of the whole board could refer any such Quaker ruling to a General Meeting of members. With future changes of the Rules being governed by a General Meeting the Rule in this form was acceptable to Friends and non-Friends alike.

A new Bill was promoted to repeal the Friends' Provident Institution Act 1915, under which the Office was first incorporated. There were a number of points in both the Act and the Rules calling for amendment to bring them into line with modern practice of the industry and the recent Insurance Companies Act 1974. There were also procedural matters, including some affecting overseas operations. These were worked out with counsel by the Office solicitor, Stanley Hewitt, and the secretary Raymond Johnson, and incorporated in the Friends' Provident Life Office Act 1975. A large contribution was made by Alfred Braithwaite, the deputy chairman, a director since 1941. It was very sad that a sudden heart attack resulted in his death when he was actually on his way to Westminster for one of the last meetings dealing with the Bill. He had been asked to stay on the board after his 70th birthday in order to see through the passing of the new Act. In his place Christopher Barber was elected deputy chairman, it being agreed at that time that as the chairman was not a Friend a deputy chairman should be appointed from amongst the Friends.

New seal and emblem adopted 1975

In January 1975 Friends' Provident Life Office opened a new chapter of the story as it led to the 150th anniversary of the foundation in 1982. After 57 years in a composite role with The Century the Office was once again a life-only mutual office. With gathering strength in the UK and Australia, and in the Fidelity in Canada, the Office was ready to be re-launched by Bill Stubbs with a management team and equipment which ensured the catching of the flood tide of events in the years ahead. The contribution brought to Friends' Provident by The Century over the years 1918–74 had been fully absorbed, and the parting left the Office facing with confidence the second major change in its history.

The corporate aim, defined in 1970, was still 'to achieve optimum controlled development, at expense levels consistent with those of the best British life-only offices'. Plans were devised with a range of new schemes to meet specialist demand in the ordinary life department, while continuing to build further the Office's reputation as a pension office.

In the course of 1975 the government's State Pension Scheme took shape, after several years of vacillation between the theories of differing political parties. There followed a very trying period during which all existing pension schemes had to be reviewed and new schemes tailor-made to meet the needs of employers, whether they opted in or out of the

State scheme. In the course of this review many of the biggest employers yielded to proposals for having the investment of self-funded pension schemes managed separately, leaving only the temporary life cover to be assured by the life offices. In order to meet this challenge Friends' Provident Managed Pension Funds Ltd was formed in 1977, using the company structure of the dormant subsidiary, English Estates Assurance Ltd, from which the outstanding business had been taken over by Friends' Provident. By this means connections with many of the Office's large pension clients were retained. The earlier performance of the unit trust and the Office's fine bonus record gave an indication of the service which the Office could give in fund management. In Ireland however legislation precluded the formation of a similar management company until the end of 1980.

Australia

Arising out of the negotiations in 1974 with the Phoenix over their acquisition of The Century discussion took place about the comparative operations of the two groups in the life market in Australia. The two operations controlled from Sydney were well matched and worked on similar agency systems. Friends' Provident was already the larger and, with the favourable climate for a mutual office in Australia, was expanding steadily, whereas the Phoenix had to concentrate on their general insurance side and were working on the consolidation of The Century in their branches. Agreement was therefore happily reached that the Office should take over the Phoenix life portfolio on 1st July 1975. Jack Lamb as general manager for Australia with Phil Burns as actuary continued as the senior executives and Phil Billings of the Phoenix assumed the important appointment of agency manager. The acquisition of this portfolio brought to the Australian account a welcome addition of mature business and a trained agency force to aid further development. At the same time a change took place in the chairmanship of the Australian Advisory Board. Sir Denzil Macarthur-Onslow retired and was succeeded by Lawford Richardson. Both these directors had given outstanding service on The Century and Friends' Provident boards for over 25 years.

In Sydney the officials and staff involved earned praise for the manner in which they handled the merger, and it was this which attracted another important opportunity to expand the development of the Office in Australia. The largest general insurance group in Australia, QBE, had decided to dispose of their life subsidiary, the Equitable Life and General Insurance Company Ltd. They had been forced to the decision by new regulations from Canberra somewhat similar in effect to those which led

Lawford Richardson, CMG, and Mrs Richardson

Sydney Harbour, NSW. FPLO chief office for Australia in foreground

to the reluctant parting of Friends' Provident and The Century. Negotiations in 1976 skilfully handled by Fred Cotton, the deputy general manager, and the Australian management, with guidance from Lawford Richardson, chairman of the Australian Advisory Board, concluded the arrangement for the Office to take over from 1st January 1977 the life portfolio of Equitable Life. As a condition for his consent to the merger the Commissioner required the actuary of the Australian series to publish annually his valuation and bonus declarations. With these two acquisitions the Office had quadrupled its Australian fund and established a self-financing branch operation ranking in the first 10 life offices in that country. In terms of ordinary life policies in force the Friends' Provident's Australian portfolio accounted in 1977 for more than 25 per cent of the volume world-wide. Thinking back to the first faltering steps in the '60s these were great achievements, and this position, coupled with the long and valuable contribution of Lawford Richardson to the Office, was recognised by his election that year as the

first overseas director on the main board in London, representing the Australian policyholders. Three years later his services to the community in New South Wales were recognised by his appointment as CMG.

The assets of the Equitable Life brought to the Office an exceptionally fine headquarters building at the northern end of Sydney Harbour Bridge, carrying considerable publicity value. Enjoying the view over the magnificent harbour and the Opera House, the chief executive of this large life-only operation is an ex-Northern general insurance man, Jack Lamb, who has given fine leadership to the Australian staff and agents since 1970.

Jack Lamb, general manager for Australia

Canada

Fidelity Life continued to make progress and earned further relaxation of the policy restraint which required expansion to be kept within the company's own resources of finance. The western provinces were however beginning to feel the strain of recession and Fidelity no longer had the support given by The Century of Canada in the sharing of the expenses of the combined headquarters for Canada in Vancouver. During 1976 and 1977 therefore, Bank of England consent was obtained to remit from London one million dollars which was the first injection of new capital since the company was purchased in 1957. This gave the company greater freedom to improve its status as a leading indigenous life office in Western Canada.

This was also a time when many of the smaller life companies in Canada were finding it increasingly difficult to develop on the traditional Canadian basis of career agents, mostly non-insurance men, recruited from other fields and supervised and trained by a branch manager who required an office and staff. Overhead costs were high and productivity and the quality of the business were too often poor. A new marketing plan was prepared by management under the president, Stewart Cunningham. This recommended that the volume and standard of the business could be improved if the branch offices were closed and regional managers were appointed to oversee the work of trained and experienced insurance general agents reporting direct to head office in Vancouver. It was a strong board, under the chairmanship of Hon Wm Hamilton, including Bill Stubbs and Fred Cotton from London, which approved in 1979 this change of organisation on a five-year trial, with a promise of necessary financial support from Friends' Provident. In 1980 the head office was moved from 1112 West Pender Street to the top floors of the prestige tower block numbered 1130, next door, built by Friends' Provident, the two buildings carrying the name Fidelity Life Centre.

Changes in Investments and Property Holding

In the five years which followed the loss of The Century the new business growth both at home and in Australia swelled the life fund and it was further expanded by the effects of general inflation. The life fund increased from £401 million in 1974 to exceed £500 million for the first time in 1976 and four years later further growth raised the figure to £851 million. Without The Century the Office's overseas investments, other than those supporting life development in Ireland, Australia and Canada, sank as low as 2.3 per cent of the total in 1977, before it was judged right to increase the portfolio in the USA. Major changes were also made in the home investment picture. In a period when industrial unrest and difficult trading conditions brought a rapid rise in interest rates equities were sold and large new holdings of gilts were acquired on very favourable terms. Holdings of mortgages on fixed rates of interest in which the Office had always been heavily invested were steadily reduced. With special encouragement from the chairman, Ted Phillips, a new move into property investment proceeded well and a vigorous specialist department managed by Bill Evans was established. Changes in the holdings and a high standard of management yielded good results, and capital appreciation in a period of fluctuating investment markets was very satisfactory.

Michael Hardie, general manager and director, investments

Coming late into the property market the Office encountered keen competition from other institutions but an outstandingly successful deal resulted from an approach to Robin Tomkins, a property developer with whom the Office had had financial dealings for some years. He was chairman of a quoted property company, Land and House Property Corporation Ltd, with which his own company Frincon Ltd had been successfully merged, leaving him a substantial shareholder. An agreed purchase of the shares of Land and House secured for the Office an important property subsidiary. Ted Phillips took the chair and Bill Stubbs, Fred Cotton and Michael Hardie were appointed directors. Robin Tomkins remained on the board bringing some of his technical staff to join the property department. The deal brought a large portfolio of property both in the UK and on the Continent with exceptionally good opportunities for making capital appreciation. The solicitor Brian Sweetland, the secretary Richard Shuker and the accountant Brian Nunn played important roles with the property department in the very large exercise involved. The experience and the strengthening of the investment department with more professional staff and technical skills provided the capability to handle other major developments or property share deals. This encouraged the taking of a stake in another public company Regional Properties Ltd, long associated with the Office.

One major property change was the very profitable sale in 1975 of 7 Leadenhall Street in the City, which had been FP & CLO's head office from 1928 to 1969, when it was registered in Dorking. A smaller but more convenient building at 7 Birchin Lane, off Cornhill in the City, was acquired to be the London office for the board and management. The other elements of head office which had remained in the City since 1957, the property and mortgage department with the legal department, and a section of the life underwriting department, were moved to Dorking, and the only staff remaining in the City were those in the Stock Exchange section of the investment department and the City branch office of which Hugh Bridgman was manager.

In the investment field the British economy was subjected to a series of crises throughout the '70s, and with variations similar conditions prevailed in other countries. The inflation rate starting at 8 per cent in 1970, soared to 25 per cent in 1975 before falling back to 8 per cent three years later, and, after severe fluctuations, rose again to 17 per cent in 1980. In these conditions interest rates rose steeply and at the peak in 1974 the yield on government stocks was over 17 per cent. There were many failures amongst companies which relied on short-term borrowing, and some larger financial companies survived only through special arrangements made by the Bank of England and the main clearing banks. The Office had little involvement in this section of the market but the general lack of confidence bore heavily on the market value of the investment portfolio overall, and violent swings on the exchange rate added to the difficulties of overseas trading. Nevertheless the combined effect of increased investment in property and high-yielding gilts secured a new record gross yield on the world-wide fund of 11.7 per cent in 1980, by which time investment markets had made a considerable though rather uncertain recovery.

Computer and Marketing Development in the UK

The period 1975–80 is the last which Friends for Life can record in detail. It was one in which real growth developed in the UK and Ireland. Even before The Century left the Group at the end of 1974 a blueprint was being prepared for a campaign far exceeding any project previously contemplated. The strategy was based on co-ordinated marketing of a new range of specialist products prepared at head office using the most up-to-date methods in the branches, with highly trained specialist staff in all areas. The Life Marketing Organisation formed under Michael Doerr in 1974 was already advancing well, but what they needed, and what they were to get, was the closest support of the computer with modern marketing techniques to make the most of their energy and resources.

Fidelity Life Centre, Vancouver, BC

*Rod Wild, assistant
general manager, systems*

Incentives were being introduced to encourage both inside and outside staff to achieve maximum productivity with minimum handling expenses.

Under the chairmanship of Fred Cotton the deputy general manager, who was elected a director in 1975, a strong Computer Steering Committee had been formed, with representation from all user departments working with management and the computer officials. After wide-ranging research into the potential use of computers by the Office the CSC decided that the equipment and service offered by IBM would best meet the Office's future requirements, rather than those of Honeywell, and the purchase of an IBM '370/145' computer was approved early in 1971. This was a big step forward, and the committee continued to show great vision and determination in planning and guiding the installation of a fully integrated computer system to handle all aspects of the work in a life and PHI operation, including the detailed functions of the accounts, renewals and agency departments.

It was a mammoth undertaking which called for great courage, and faith in the future, and was given full support by the directors. It became clear, however, by 1974 that the size and sophisticated nature of the computer operations called for a greater measure of expertise than could be expected from the staff seconded from other departments. This was first found by the engagement of Rod Wild whose outstanding ability was derived from an exceptional background, with wide and varied experience of major projects. As manager of the computer services department he recruited other experts to bring greater strength to the existing department. Under the direction of the CSC and in partnership with the user departments the new team planned and developed the first four-year programme, an operation which was succinctly summarised by Rod Wild in a report to the Board:

> 'A study team, drawn from the management of the Office, has recommended an uncompromisingly modern system. This would use television-style terminals and remote printers in both branches and Head Office. Nearly all transactions would be entered to the computer system directly. Most paper processes would be abolished.'

This heralded the startling innovation which appeared in 1975 called the Generalised Life Assurance Data Inquiry System, known familiarly by the appealing code name GLADIS. It was envisaged that over a four-year period all operations for new business in the ordinary life and PHI departments, followed in due course by the pensions department, and all policy management, with the accounts, renewals and agency records would be brought into the system. Push-button control would be

GLADIS terminal first link-up January 1976 by Bill Stubbs at West End branch, watched by Rod Wild and Tom Muir

available to management and to head office and branch users. On 18th January 1976 the first quotation on GLADIS was processed by Bill Stubbs at West End branch. This development was quickly expanded, all branches in the UK and Ireland being linked to head office within the year. Normal ordinary life policies could be underwritten and printed from terminals in the branches to be issued, fully recorded in the computer, within a few minutes of an enquiry being received. Enthusiasm at both head office and branches ensured immediate success for GLADIS, which was reflected in the volume of new business and in the enhancement of the reputation of the Office, particularly amongst brokers. A search on the terminals by the branch or underwriter gave full information on a policyholder and his policies, and details of an agent's account, when premium collection and renewals had been brought in, with an optical word-input system.

In 1978 under the code name PATSY the computer took over the mass of detail involved in payment of pensions and annuities. The following year saw the birth of another important lady, ROSIE, designed to handle quotations and the issue and annual review of all group schemes in the pensions and PHI departments other than the largest pension schemes, which are to be brought in later.

Possible developments remained under constant review, such as

137

experiments made with portable terminals which can be used through any domestic or Post Office telephone working to the branch or head office, and colour has been introduced to facilitate reading on the terminal screens. A business systems unit studied clerical procedures in general and introduced large-scale microfilming and also word-processing machines linked to the computer, which can take over much of the stereotyped work of the ordinary typewriter. The whole operation has most impressive ongoing features, based on the principle that the computer should be used as far as possible for all branch filing and head office records. In 1980 the board authorised the replacement of the main computer by a new model IBM '3033' to handle the anticipated load from developments already approved. Great success has been achieved exceeding expectations of cost savings and efficiency. Extensive further improvement can be expected with confidence. Rod Wild, appointed assistant general manager in 1980, dreams of a paperless insurance company, but a blind eye would have to be turned to the lorry loads of salvage paper leaving by the back door.

In close liaison with the Computer Steering Committee the Life Marketing Organisation, under Mike Doerr who was appointed a general manager in 1980, had completely overhauled the agency, marketing and publicity methods, both at head office and in the branches. Malcolm Payne, brought from Birmingham to Dorking as production manager, directed new business, recruitment and training in the branches. He had strong technical support from head office where an extensive programme of training for both producers and clerical staff was arranged to raise the standard of specialist skills required. The LMO in conjunction with the actuarial department reviewed all the contracts offered by the life, pensions and PHI departments, shaping new schemes, such as 'Maxidowment', 'Multidowment' and 'Friends Flexible Savings Plan', which carried the FPLO specialist brand mark, and brought a rich harvest in both premium income and the number of new policies. The pensions department held its position as a leader in its field, and the PHI department saw very good results especially for the group schemes. To co-ordinate these plans a new Marketing Project Committee was formed, with representation from the agency, actuarial and computer services departments, to meet top management and branch representatives to study market moves by competitors which could be quickly matched or bettered. By these means the Office went out to woo brokers and major agents and earned their growing support as the new contracts, technical advice and speed of service, came to be recognised throughout the country.

The reaction in the branches to the installation of the GLADIS terminals continued to be enthusiastic. It gave the branch managers a measure of control of underwriting which they had always wanted, and also the ability to give unsurpassed service to their clients. They recognised the new tools and new skills which they could use to improve productivity to meet, or exceed, the challenging targets set. The clerical staff at branches also found a new interest in their contribution to the success of the branch. Without the load of record keeping, and with far less correspondence to be handled, the total clerical staff at branches did not need to be increased at all in the years 1974–81. The number of inspectors rose by 50 per cent and the number of ordinary life and PHI policies handled in the UK and Ireland went up from 36,348 in 1974 to a target figure of 70,000 for 1981. Some rearrangement of branch areas took place, and between 1972 and 1981 the number of branches was increased from 20 to 30.

Producers and clerical staff responded to a well prepared system of personal and branch competitions, related to targets and budgets, which carried attractive rewards for individual and branch success. Interest was fanned by a new *Branch Lines* magazine which wrote up the performance of successful competitors for the titles of the Branch of the Year or the Inspector of the Year, and in other competitions such as the '150 Club' for those who exceeded their targets for the year by more than 50 per cent. Altogether these and other stimulants reinforced by production conferences and progressive training raised to a high level the standards and practice of life insurance marketing. In 1979 a special competition gave the winning branch managers, superintendents and inspectors, with their wives, an invitation to attend a sales convention in Bermuda. The value and popularity of this project has ensured very keen interest in a similar convention in the 150th anniversary year in 1982, with Barbados as the chosen location.

New ideas on publicity were successfully introduced in the late '70s. The traditional and expensive advertisements in national and provincial newspapers were almost eliminated, and the whole range of publicity material was redesigned to high standards, colourful and arresting for direct approach to brokers and agents. A short trial on Southern Region television commercial channel in 1976 gave poor value, and was abandoned. In 1980, however, the Office entered into a sponsorship agreement with the Badminton Association of England, which brought prestige advertising of Friends' Provident to both clubs and players. It also gives several hours of prime television coverage each year. The greatest success was the institution, under the name Friends' Provident Masters Badminton Tournament, of the original open world-wide championship played at the Albert Hall in London in September 1979, 1980 and again in 1981.

In head office and the branches morale was high and there was justifiable pride in the results achieved in the seven years, 1974–80, of the marketing and computer combined operation, which are shown in the statistics in Appendix IV. It was a strategic success made possible by the close co-operation of all concerned. All the head office departments had accepted, and undertaken most commendably, considerable changes in their roles and administrative functions. Careful research followed each new development of products and systems in the market so that the Office could be ready in its own time to make tactical or strategical changes. But with the momentum of progress so well maintained, in the broker market especially, it was clearly right to keep closely to the principle of reinforcing success. It should be remembered that the Office throughout this period had been increasing its share of the market in the UK and Ireland at a time of major recession when rampant inflation and rising costs bedevilled all trade and industry. In years of very difficult investment conditions the actuary Doug King, who was appointed a general manager in 1980, was able to recommend in 1976 a reversionary bonus on the main series of £4.40 per cent with the terminal bonus at 20 per cent. In 1979 these rates were increased to £4.75 per cent and 30 per cent respectively.

At the end of 1980 an agreement of outstanding importance was made with Goudse Insurance Company of Holland, the parent office of the English brokers, Endsleigh Insurance Services Ltd. The Office acquired a one-third holding of the shares of Endsleigh from Goudse, and a tied agency agreement was concluded with the brokers. The Office had enjoyed a close relationship with this firm, which specialises in the needs of university students and staff, since its earliest days as a subsidiary of the National Union of Students in the '60s. Under the agreement, which came into effect on 1st January 1981, all Endsleigh's conventional life business comes to the Office. The quality of their business is undoubtedly very good, and the potential growth in their special fields is enormous. For Endsleigh, top grade service, including a special terminal linked by GLADIS to the computer, will give them not only speed of service and reduced expenses, but in their head office at Cheltenham their officials are authorised to exercise powers similar to those of a Friends' Provident branch manager, with prescribed authority for underwriting and issue of policies. It was by virtue of Endsleigh's direct connection with the students and staff of the Universities that such an arrangement could be made with mutual benefit without in any way prejudicing the Office's important connections with other insurance brokers whose support of Friends' Provident had increased steadily particularly during the years 1975–80.

For the PHI department under Frank Martin the second half of the '70s was a period of steady growth, stimulated by changes which affected the

Mike Doerr, general manager and director, operations

department in those years. First the closure of Edinburgh Centre brought the department to Dorking in closer touch with senior management and the planning team of the LMO, and also nearer to the brokers in London. Secondly, after the loss of The Century, PHI policies were written in the Friends' Provident name and jointly marketed in the vigorous production campaigns of the life and pensions departments. Thirdly the department benefited at an early date from the improved service offered by both GLADIS and ROSIE computer operations.

The progress measured in premium income in the UK and Ireland was a 100 per cent increase between 1971 and 1975 and a further 250 per cent in 1980 over the 1975 total. Some of this success was undoubtedly due to the effect of inflation on salaries, but it was achieved in the UK in the face of strong and growing competition. Group schemes were developed with brokers and in 1979 a profit sharing group scheme was introduced on terms attractive to employers. This innovation recalled the ambitious but short-lived survival bonus offered in some of the original policies issued by the Sickness and Accident Assurance Association when they first introduced the non-cancellable sickness and accident policy to the market in 1885.

In Australia development of the PHI account had been held up for several years by a difficulty arising out of the Commonwealth tax regulations. This was overcome and in 1980 a start was made to develop PHI business in earnest with most encouraging initial success.

In 1981 another innovation was a link between the Office and Western Provident Association of Bristol, one of the leading private health and hospitalisation societies. By an agreement with the WPA any Friends' Provident PHI policyholder is entitled to enjoy membership of the WPA Supercover Plans for himself and his family with a 40 per cent reduction in the subscription. Such a combination of permanent health and private health insurance had not previously been offered in the UK. It is a natural linkage between the best precautions to prevent or minimise incapacity with insurance to cover the cost if earnings are jeopardised by sickness or accident.

Chapter 9

Looking Forward 1981

THE STORY OF Friends for Life must be closed in 1981 so that this book can be published in time for the 150th anniversary year in 1982. A glance back over half a century, well within the memories of a large number of pensioners, will recall in stark contrast the conditions in 1931, which led in 1935 to the hunger march from Jarrow to Westminster. The full shock of the Depression which had started in the US in 1929 had reached Britain, the Commonwealth and Europe. For FP & CLO it was a major crisis. Over 60 per cent of the Century's general business was written in US and Canada and the losses there and elsewhere were disastrous. The Office was heavily over-invested in dollars and an overall depreciation of 50 per cent on the life fund at the end of 1931 revealed a shortfall of 5·3 per cent of assets to cover liabilities, with total Group funds standing at £7.28 million. New life premium income fell by 55 per cent in 1931, a large part being single premiums and annuity considerations. Friends' Provident was looking towards its centenary year but plans for marking the occasion, including a special life bonus, were cancelled. Older pensioners well remember the 10 per cent cut in the majority of salaries with no increases for the four years 1931–34.

In 1981 the Office, in common with other insurers, has again been taking for five years and more the buffeting of a world-wide recession in which the industry and commerce of all Western nations have been shaken almost as violently as they were in 1931, but the slower onset, and more closely linked international control, made survival easier. For Friends' Provident wider dimensions and greater stability enabled the Office to ride the storms and shape its course for further progress. It is

Fred Cotton, chief general manager and director

143

however a constant and continuing struggle against the effects of inflation on new developments, on expenses and on investment policy, and the records achieved are the rewards of great effort and resourcefulness. In 1980 world-wide new annual premiums increased by 12 per cent to £30 million and single premiums at £16.7 million rose by 44 per cent. For the Group new life sums assured reached a new record at £1,192 million.

In the UK the continuing successful campaign by the Life Marketing Organisation, backed by expanded and new programmes devised and operated by the Computer Steering Committee, maintains the impetus of growth for the decade. In the ordinary life and PHI departments new products met with success which justified a further increase in the number of producers and the opening of five new branches in 1981. The pensions department retained their firm hold on the market, with inflation helping them with increased salaries in one way, but on the other hand reducing the market by closures and redundancies. The Managed Pensions Funds company shows progress, with the new Irish company making a good start.

In Ireland a new manager for the republic, Ian Farr FFA, was appointed to oversee the three branches at Dublin, Cork and Galway. This gave a closer identity with the Republic for the Office's special position there. The ordinary life and PHI results were good but the recession brought a reduction in new pensions business.

In Australia under Jack Lamb expansion continues with a 9.7 per cent increase in premium income in 1980 including improved results in the pensions department and a good start in the new PHI contracts introduced in 1979. Lawford Richardson who had been chairman of the Australian Advisory Board since 1975 and a member of that board for 29 years reached retirement age and was succeeded by Peter Watson DFC, the deputy chairman.

Fidelity Life in Canada entered 1981 with renewed vigour derived from their regional managing agency system which replaced the branch organisation, giving advantages in both management and control of expenses. Stewart Cunningham the president was joined by a newly recruited vice-president Brian Douthwaite as director of agencies to supervise the new development. The company continued to derive strength from the board under the chairmanship of Hon Wm Hamilton.

The Group total invested funds rose from £350 million in 1971 to £1,096 million in 1981. It was a period of unceasing difficulties in the investment markets both in the UK and overseas, in which the growing paralysis of industry and commerce by inflation and related industrial and political crises had brought world markets to a state of a major depression. The Office's equity portfolio had performed well, but the

John Robson: 90th birthday party at Dorking F. Cotton, Mrs Marjorie Tapscott, J. Robson, P. Leishman, W. Palmer and D. Tregoning

major feature was the chance to take advantage of the historically very high rates of interest obtained from gilt-edged and other fixed interest securities. This and the yield obtained on the large new portfolio of property investments, with a reduction in the holdings of mortgages, resulted in an increase of the gross interest on the rapidly growing fund from 7.59 per cent in 1971 to 11.70 per cent in 1980. The actuary Doug King was thus able to increase in 1981 the terminal bonus, introduced at 20 per cent in 1969, to the record level of 40 per cent of maturity and attached bonuses. It is a strong position which is carried forward for the next reversionary bonus declaration at the end of 1982 and despite the continuing strain of the depression it must encourage with-profit policyholders who have enjoyed the fruits of the Friends' Provident's high bonus record over the past 25 years. An equally strong position prevails in the segregated Staff Pensions Fund to which major transfers have been made in recent years enabling the trustees to allow for the foreseeable effect of inflation on the pensions which members of the staff can expect to enjoy. Those already on pension have greatly appreciated what the directors have done to help them with improvements in the pensions for themselves and for widows.

145

The computer marches on

In the power house of the computer room the Computer Steering Committee kept the expanding programmes moving in the second four-year plan. These involved particularly bringing into the GLADIS and ROSIE systems major schemes in the pensions and PHI departments and a great deal of detail for executive benefit schemes. Older systems have been regularly overhauled and new developments introduced, with far-sighted research projects being constantly undertaken. With commendable regularity the department has kept to its forecasts and budgeting of dates and savings in both expenses and staff. By the success of GLADIS the clerical staff working on routine duties at head office and in the branches has been reduced by more than 10 per cent without redundancies, during a period when the volume of business handled was greatly increased and new branches were opened. In May 1981 Rod Wild had the distinction of being invited by IBM to read a paper to their International Insurance Forum in Florida, this being only the second time that such an invitation had been extended to a guest from Europe, a tribute to what he and his colleagues had achieved at Dorking.

Board and management changes

In the years 1980 and 1981 there were a number of changes in the board of directors and in senior management. At the beginning of 1980 Bill Stubbs as the chief executive was given the title of chief general manager and his deputy Fred Cotton that of deputy chief general manager. The next three senior executives Doug King the actuary, Michael Hardie, investments manager, and Mike Doerr, marketing manager, were all advanced to be general managers and joined Bill Stubbs and Fred Cotton as executive directors. This changed the traditional composition of the board which then consisted of five executive and 10 non-executive directors of whom five Friends comprised the minimum requirement under the Rules. Four new assistant general managers were appointed: Colin McWilliam, personnel, Malcolm Payne, marketing, Peter Silvester, pensions and Rod Wild, systems.

In January 1981 Paul Honigmann who had been appointed a director in 1979 resigned on personal grounds. In May at the AGM Lawford Richardson was succeeded by Peter Watson, to represent the Australian members who, in terms of their policies in force, by this time represented approximately 25 per cent of the total. At the same meeting Bill Stubbs retired, and was succeeded in the appointment of chief general manager by Fred Cotton. Stubbs had asked to be allowed to retire early so that he

could return to Vancouver BC which had been the adopted home for himself and his family for over 30 years, since he emigrated from Sheffield to Canada after war service in the RAF. He joined The Century there in 1964 as assistant manager for Canada with the intention that he should succeed Harry Cutler as manager for Canada. After $3\frac{1}{2}$ years however he was appointed general manager for Australia. After only two years there the tragic death of Dewi Lloyd Humphreys in 1970 led to his being appointed chief assistant general manager at head office in anticipation of the retirement of David Tregoning in 1973. Bill Stubbs' appointment as general manager was the shortest of any service by a chief executive of Friends' Provident, but while he was at the helm he steered a course through some of the most difficult channels in the history of the Office. He handled with great ability the negotiations for the sale of The Century which changed the whole character of the Office as it reverted, after 56 years as a composite organisation, to being once again a life-only mutual office. He then advanced from strength in the UK to consolidate Friends' Provident as a leading British office in Australia,

Friends' Provident Masters Badminton final, Royal Albert Hall, London, 1980

The chairman with Air Vice-Marshal G. Lamb, chief executive of the Badminton Association of England, who opened the Sports Centre at Dorking 2nd June 1981

and to re-organise the Canadian subsidiary Fidelity Life in Vancouver. Both at home and overseas Bill Stubbs brought fresh enthusiasm and new vigour in his direction of what was in effect the relaunching of Friends' Provident. The closely co-ordinated campaigns of the Life Marketing Organisation with the outstanding contribution of the Computer Steering Committee in the UK and Ireland brought success which has given a new dimension to the standing of the Office amongst the British mutual life offices. With the directness of Yorkshire and Canada mingled in his thinking and with his sense of humour and in his way of life he gave leadership and clarity of decision which were recognised by all his colleagues, both directors and staff.

Fred Cotton carries on the same forward-looking policy, developing projects in which he has already played a major part. From the time when he joined the Office in 1959 he has had wide experience in the pensions and overseas life and systems departments. Before he became assistant general manager in 1971 he had been seconded for two years as deputy general manager of Fidelity Life in Vancouver, and taken charge of the investment department for a period in 1970 following the death of Reginald Harding. He was soon marked down for a senior executive position, and his contribution to the major recent events, particularly the sale of The Century and the acquisition of the Australian life portfolios of the Phoenix and the Equitable Life, brought him recognition in the industry. In the Office too, his chairmanship of the Computer Steering Committee ensured results from the close liaison between the systems executives and the actuaries and accountants with

The Garden Fête at Pixham End, Dorking, June 1981

the user departments and the branches. He has the distinction of being the first actuary qualified by examination to be the chief executive of Friends' Provident. It is certainly with the fullest confidence that his colleagues both at home and overseas play their parts with him in meeting the growing challenge of the future.

In years of peace and war, prosperity and recession, Friends' Provident, like a well found and happy ship, has weathered storm and calm, foul wind and fair. As the story of *Friends for Life* is brought to its close the clouds of severe world-wide recession, darkened by inflation and industrial unrest, are slow to clear. The way ahead may be rough and hard but the record to the end of 1981 shows that the Office is able to maintain the momentum of its progress. New technology and exciting new equipment auger well for plans now being developed.

Fred Cotton with guidance from Ted Phillips and the board is directing a team which has in depth an exceptionally high standard of professional and technical skills. Inspired by success they have the courage and the will to go forward, and can take their password from Longfellow's lines:

'A youth who bore 'mid snow and ice
A banner with the strange device
*   "Excelsior".'*

149

Conclusion

OUR STORY HAS taken us from the Pennines in 1831 to Box Hill in 1981. The journey has not been uneventful. In the course of 150 years the modest Friendly Society formed solely for the benefit of members of a small dissenting sect has developed into a leading British mutual life assurance office having close on 500,000 ordinary life and PHI policyholders with a large membership in Ireland and Australia, and a strong subsidiary company in Western Canada. In the list of British life offices Friends' Provident ranks fifteenth in terms of its assets. Of the mutuals it comes fifth. Among the 'Five Societies' formed under the Friendly Societies Act 1829 it is the largest of the four that have survived. Countless thousands have benefited from its policies and the bonuses paid under them. All this could not have been achieved without the devoted service of generations of men and women who have worked for the Office; but devoted service is not in itself enough. The ship must not only be manned; it must be kept on the right course. On occasion the economic climate will force changes. The choice and timing of such changes means the difference between success and failure.

For the first 85 years the course seemed clear. The mission was to cater for the Quaker community. That community has always remained small, never exceeding 22,000 adult members, and the market became saturated. Successive relaxations extended the eligibility for policies to the relatives and friends of Quakers, and even to those who had attended Quaker schools, but the danger of stagnation remained, and a business that cannot grow is all too apt to decay. Staff and agents look for alternative employment that will bring greater job satisfaction and rewards.

Early in the 20th century the large fire insurance companies adopted a policy of diversification by acquiring the business of specialist companies in the accident, marine and life fields. These takeovers were invariably by agreement. The Friends' Provident itself discussed in 1912 the possibility of selling out to the Royal Exchange Assurance. Nothing came of this directly, though the discussions were to have an indirect sequel of great moment because they brought Henry Tapscott, Birmingham branch manager of the Royal Exchange, to the notice of the board. The possibility of a merger with the Sceptre Life was also considered but in the event that office joined the Eagle Star in 1917. It was clear that something should be done, but what?

World War I was a testing time for small life offices. A check to the flow of new business coupled with staff shortages and depreciation of their investments led a dozen of them into surrender of their identity in the years 1917–23, including the Clergy Mutual, the oldest of the 'Five Societies'. Most joined composite groups. Friends' Provident surprised the British market by itself acquiring The Century Insurance Company Ltd in 1918. By this one step the Office changed its form and character and was assured of a future which might otherwise have been in doubt.

It was a brilliant move and one marked by novelty as the first occasion when a mutual life office acquired a general insurance company. The merger proved to be beneficial to all parties. Mergers are not always successful but in this case there was a strong element of symbiosis. If Henry Tapscott had done nothing else for the Friends' Provident he would have earned an honoured place in its history by his success in the delicate negotiations that led to the merger. In fact he did a great deal more.

A char-à-banc, one van and one private car sufficed to bring the Friends' Provident staff and records from Bradford to London in 1919 to the new head office. The Institution ceased in 1915 to serve Quakers alone. Until Henry Tapscott's arrival in 1916 the board and the staff had consisted entirely of Quakers but a process of secularisation set in when two directors from The Century joined the board, and a branch network staffed almost entirely by Century men and women was established. The fluctuations in fortune that are inseparable from a small general account made for a bumpy ride. Henry Tapscott deplored the tendency in North America to rely on investment income rather than underwriting profits in general insurance, but he found in the end that there was no choice. Just as his early problems appeared to have been resolved the life business too was hit by the world depression of the early '30s. For a brief period even survival might have been in question. Liabilities exceeded assets at the time of the centenary and the special centenary bonus announced in advance in 1930 had to be cancelled.

The troubles were happily short-lived. A resourceful investment policy yielded good results and the Office was well placed to face the shock of the 1939 war although bonuses had again to be postponed. Henry Tapscott saw out the war and handed over a going concern to Douglas Pringle, recruited from the Guardian Assurance Company who, even before his appointment as chief executive, took a leading role in preparing far-sighted plans for the post-war period which he was then able to implement. Douglas Pringle can best be judged by the strength of the organisation and management team which he built up in the post-war years. His was the courageous project to move the head office to Dorking. This was done some years before the exodus of insurance companies from the City became general. The move, carried out by his successor, proved an unqualified success. In management as in investment it is correct timing that yields the best results.

David Tregoning's term as chief executive illustrates the flexibility needed for the management of a large business. His war-time experience gave him an appreciation of the need for systematic planning, the importance of recruiting and training leaders and technicians, and an understanding of the difference between strategy and tactics. Events forced certain changes such as the rationalisation of the decentralised branch system and the withdrawal from the USA and Africa, but these retreats were more than compensated by the development of life assurance in Canada and Australia.

In retrospect the separation of life and general branches in the UK, though not undertaken with the abandonment of general insurance in mind, provided a strong base for life development required by his successor, Bill Stubbs, when Friends' Provident found no option to the sale of The Century in 1974. Once again the form and future of the Office were changed basically, revealing new potential objectives on the road ahead.

The new, trimmer, Life Office, had, of course, plenty of problems of its own, but no one was better equipped to tackle them than Bill Stubbs with his experience of organising branch and field staff in Canada and Australia. The achievements of the years since 1974, with the wholehearted acceptance of bold computerisation by all concerned, and above all by the Life Marketing Organisation, are the best evidence of Bill Stubbs' success in management. Fred Cotton, the first actuary qualified by examination to be chief executive, takes over a business in far better shape than anyone could have foreseen in 1974, well equipped to weather the economic blizzard that is blowing as he assumes command.

Friends' Provident has over its 150 years demonstrated an ability to ride out storms and maintain its independence. Its most difficult times were those that affected other offices as well: World War I, the depression of the 1930s, World War II, the underwriting crisis of 1957, and the events that led up to the separation from The Century in 1974.

For any business organisation the first requirement is to survive and Friends' Provident has always demonstrated its ability to do this and more, even when survival has meant drastic adaptation. Mutual life assurance is based on the concept that the enterprise exists for the benefit of those policyholders who participate in the profits, but a broad view has to be taken as to who are such policyholders. It includes not only the current ones who might argue, as they used to, that their pockets would be best lined by restricting or even stopping the flow of new business so that their fund would show steadily rising profits for them alone. The view has everywhere been preferred, however, that a mutual life office exists for the benefit of both present and future policyholders, and that it is intrinsically good to spread the availability of life assurance as widely as possible. The extension of activities to a separate but dependent fund in Australia can be justified on this ground. Employees of mutual life offices too are entitled to expect that expansion shall be planned so that they may have fair scope to develop their careers and earning power to the full extent that is compatible with the office's primary duty to its policyholders. Keeping a proper balance between the interests of all generations of policyholders and those of the staff is, and must continue to be, the preoccupation of the board of any mutual life office. The dominant position achieved by mutuals in the USA, Canada and Australia demonstrates that there is still a great future for mutual life assurance. In that future Friends' Provident is well equipped and ready to play a leading part, in the UK and Ireland, and in Australia.

Acknowledgments

THE AUTHORS WOULD like to thank those who have given generously of their time and experience in the research and preparation of this book. First they thank the chairman, Ted Phillips, and the directors of Friends' Provident Life Office for making available the facilities for the research and clerical work to be done at Dorking. The management secretaries and technicians in the life department each did her stint converting tregoningraphy into fair typed copy for the word-processor – to them our thanks.

For the detail of the story and of the personalities in the period 1900–65, including those of The Century, the clarity of John Robson's memory, in his 90th year, was a great source of inspiration. Mrs Henry Tapscott recalled events in Bradford and the early days in London.

Senior executive officials, especially Bill Stubbs, Fred Cotton and Doug King gave considerable assistance in correcting and improving the text of more recent periods.

Line managers at Dorking and others including pensioners were encouraging with their interest and help. The same enthusiasm was found in Sydney and Vancouver. John Murphy and the publicity department were very helpful in the preparation of the illustrations.

Credit must be given to Francis Granville, whose keen sense of history brought together much of the earliest material of the 19th century on which research was based, and which is the foundation of the unusually complete archives of the Office. The greatest contribution has been made by Muriel Hayman whose inherited interest and long career in the Office have flourished with dedication and accuracy to make her an ideal research companion. She leaves her mark not only on the text and illustrations of this book, but also on the collation and indexing of the archives at Dorking.

Gordon McKee, the headmaster, and Kenneth Limb, the bursar, welcomed us to the birthplace of Friends' Provident Institution at Ackworth School when the school was celebrating its bicentenary in 1979. A deep debt of gratitude must also be paid to Ted Milligan and Malcolm Thomas, the librarians at Friends House in London. Their scholarship and great fund of detailed information about Quakers and individual Friends were freely and enthusiastically made available for the authors.

154

Appendices

Appendix I Part 1

The Society of Friends

The Christian community, called the Society of Friends since the latter part of the 18th century, was originally known as The Quakers. Their background was in the turbulent years of political strife and civil war which led to the establishment of Oliver Cromwell's Presbyterian regime. The Puritan movement was large and strong, but within it there were a number of dissenters who were strongly opposed to the rigid religious discipline and narrow doctrine of the day. Independent sects sprang up under a number of different names, such as Baptists, Ranters, Levellers and Seekers. Among these the Quakers in the middle of the 17th century found a strong following particularly in the north of England. They met together for worship, not for formal prayer or preaching, but waited in silence for inspiration, feeling the universal presence of Christ to guide those who believed in Him. As anything arose in the mind of anyone, of any age or either sex, so a member would speak or read a passage of the bible or other books or writing. They saw no need for any special church building or for doctrinal liturgy, believing that out of a concentrated and expectant silence God might use any one of the worshippers as a minister of truth. There was no form of priesthood as such but anyone of either sex who showed special merit in oral or written testimony was recognised in the Meeting as an elder or a minister.

Local gatherings became known as Preparative Meetings, a number of these being grouped together as a Monthly Meeting. These again were linked together as Quarterly Meetings covering one or more counties. When the organisation was fully established the Quarterly Meetings recognised the authority of one Yearly Meeting in London. Ministers or

London Published by R. Ackermann Repository of Arts. 101 Strand Oct.r 1807

QUAKERS MERRY MAKING.

leaders would visit other Meetings and join in their worship which made them seem, as indeed they thought themselves, very similar in nature to the earliest Christian churches to which St Paul preached and wrote. Amongst these early leaders George Fox (1624–91) proved himself pre-eminent. From the age of 19 he toured the country, first seeking guidance from other left-wing sectarian groups, and later offering his initiative in both religious learning and the organisation and administration of Meetings throughout the UK. In this way stability was given to the growing community which was recognised a century later as The Society of Friends.

Quakerism spread rapidly especially in the North of England and was linked with Meetings formed in London and many of the major cities and towns in England. After the Restoration in 1660 however new

*Quakers Merry Making,
early 19th-century
cartoon*

157

The Gracechurch Meeting
c 1770

difficulties arose. Stubborn reaction to laws or regulations which conflicted with their beliefs or practice soon brought the Quakers into sharp conflict with authority and other religious communities. This led to persecution in many forms, consolidated in the Quakers Act 1662, which imposed many restrictions and penalties on those who did not conform with the statutory obligation to attend Church or pay tithes. This Act was not repealed until 1689, by the Toleration Act, and by that time Quakers had suffered no less than 15,000 penal sentences and more than 450 had died in prison. These were large figures from a small community. Under the Corporation Act 1661, Quakers with other dissenters were banned from any public office, and also from entry to Oxford or Cambridge Universities.

Many Quakers sought refuge from religious persecution in America. Amongst these William Penn, who had been imprisoned in England several times for his religious views, took a leading part in the settlement and early administration of Pennsylvania. The constitution of this state was originally drawn up on Quaker principles of tolerance and practice. George Fox wrote to Friends in America suggesting that they should set up an organisation of Meetings similar to that in the UK and by the end of the 17th century Yearly Meetings had been established in six states. Although these were independent of each other, they all recognised the parent body in London. The Society of Friends, therefore, at the beginning of the 18th century had established in the UK and America an entity as a church in the modern sense, and by strict adherence to their principles and way of life earned wide respect and acceptance amongst the more tolerant in an age of religious differences.

The Quaker code of behaviour was basically one of self-discipline, strengthened by the surveillance of the individual's actions under the scrutiny of fellow members of the Meeting. Quakers held no general creed but looked in all things for the guidance of the Holy Spirit supported by their reading of the bible and the published writings of Friends. The minutes, or Epistles, of the Quarterly or Yearly Meetings were distributed. These included, in addition to religious guidance, many matters of personal behaviour such as plainness in dress and speech, and also temperance and modesty in social intercourse. The Epistles dealt in some detail with the manner in which a Friend should conduct his trade or business, insisting on the keeping of regular accounts and paying debts promptly and the avoidance of any dishonest practice. A committee would be formed to help a Friend in difficulty, and bring him back on to the road if he had strayed. Similar action might be taken if a Friend were to ignore the exhortation that he, or she, should not marry a non-Quaker. A committee of the Meeting would visit the errant suitor and the family, and try to prevent the marriage.

John Bright MP, leading reformer, and a close friend of Benjamin Ecroyd

Scrupulous honesty and fair dealing in goods of the best quality and material brought customers to the Quaker shops and warehouses and Quakers' competent handling of their own financial affairs led to other people seeking their advice in the role of bankers. There were few wealthy members other than those who had acquired money by their success in farming, industry or trade. Indeed it was said in Quaker circles that 'a carriage and pair does not long continue to drive to a Meeting House'. On the other hand the number of Quakers in the poorer section of the community was small. Despite the accepted obligation to help those in need, poor Friends were urged to maintain themselves and their family by 'frugality and industry'. Great importance was attached to education for both boys and girls and in places such as Ackworth, York, Bristol and Reading, first-class Quaker schools were established and maintain today their high reputation. After leaving school, however, as Friends were not able to go to Oxford or Cambridge until 1871, they tended to go into business or a profession at any early age, and in family firms their energy and inventiveness was often given full rein.

Old and young men and women mingled at Quarterly and Yearly Meetings and when they travelled on business they would be offered hospitality by Friends in another area. In this way discussion on farming methods, industrial development, scientific and medical research would help in the serious advancement of a young man in his trade or profession. This practice also led to a wider field for intermarriage amongst Friends. During the 18th and 19th centuries the Society

Meeting House, built 1710, at Come-to-Good, Truro, Cornwall, still used for worship in 1982

produced a number of major family dynasties which, by partnerships and co-operation, attained considerable strength and produced great leaders in industry and commerce and achieved much by applying their energy to social reform. Their contribution to financial and industrial development and to local and national social welfare far exceeded what might have been expected from their membership in the UK. After standing at 18,000 at the end of the 18th century the adult membership declined to 16,000 by 1860. After that it rose again to 20,000 a century later, but in recent years has again dropped by about 20 per cent

In the United States a number of new independent State Yearly Meetings were formed and in Australia, South Africa and Central America also Yearly Meetings of Friends were established. Amongst those who were sent to encourage these new Meetings was Joseph Dymond, the secretary and chief executive of FPI, who was given leave of absence on two occasions to go as a minister to Friends in the Australian colonies in 1873, and to America and Canada in 1874.

The strongest Quaker principles are pursuit of peace and abhorrence of war. In this they have been inspired by the declaration of George Fox and other leading Quakers in 1661 – 'We utterly deny all outward wars and strife and fightings with outward weapons for any end, or under any pretence whatsoever'. Their pacifism brought them persecution and imprisonment even in the two world wars of the 20th century, although by that time there were Friends who served in the armed forces as combatants, some with distinction, while others served in noncombatant roles. Many joined Friends' Ambulance Units working with the forces on active service or Friends' Relief Services with the civilian authorities. Quaker relief work has been recognised in many parts of the world since late in the 18th century. In recent years the British Friends' Service Council, co-operating with the American Friends' Service Committee, has done a great deal to help those who suffered from war or other disasters as was recognised in 1947 by the award of the Nobel Peace Prize. In many countries of the world the Friends' Service Council finds scope for medical and educational work amongst the emerging nations. From the earliest days of George Fox's ministry Friends have taken a leading part in the abolition of slavery, not only in the British Commonwealth and America, but also in other countries where the practice of slavery still persists to a surprising extent.

Joseph Pease, first Quaker MP, father of Joseph Pease FPI director

Friends' political activities have been largely concerned with movements for social justice such as the abolition of capital punishment and penal reform. Prison visiting was led by Elizabeth Fry, and an increasing number of Friends were active in movements demanding equal rights for women in society. The abolition of the Test and Corporation Acts in 1828 and 1829 allowed affirmation instead of the Oath of Allegiance and so lifted the ban on Quakers holding public office, enabling them to stand in local and parliamentary elections. In 1833, one year after the passing of the Reform Act, Joseph Pease, whose son Joseph was a director of FPI (1867–71), became the first Friend to be a member of Parliament. He was distinguished by his appearance in the House in the traditional Quaker broad brimmed hat and cloak. He was joined by the very active reformer John Bright. In all about 70 Friends have sat in the House of Commons. Others, including Lord Seebohm, and Lord Taylor of Gryfe, have used their special talents in the House of Lords. In the main Friends tended to hold Liberal views but to sit as independents rather than as members of tightly disciplined political machines. It is probably in international affairs and welfare that Friends have distinguished themselves most in politics.

Throughout the 18th and 19th centuries Friends took an increasingly active part in the temperance movement. Well brewed ale was a normal drink for all classes when water was liable to be polluted and the water-borne scourges of cholera and typhoid were often epidemic. Throughout the country a number of Quaker families had taken part in the brewing industry, but in the 1830s many of them such as the Seebohms, Ellises and the Priestmans, amongst the founders of FPI, were turning over to woollen or other industries. A strict discipline was also applied to the use of tobacco and other forms of indulgence. The resultant improved expectation of life undoubtedly earned the special terms and bonuses which FPI was able to offer during the years up to 1915 when membership was confined entirely to members of the Society of Friends and their relatives or associates.

There were several industries in which Quaker names, generally in family businesses, came to be known world-wide. The first which comes to mind is probably the chocolate industry in which Rowntree of York, Cadbury of Birmingham and Fry of Bristol are household names. In the biscuit industry Huntley & Palmer of Reading, Carr of Carlisle, with Jacobs of Dublin, all had Quaker origins and came to be amalgamated in Associated Biscuit Manufacturers Limited. Quaker families also formed the large chemical company Albright and Wilson in Birmingham with which is associated the Bryant & May Match Company of Gloucester.

A long list could be compiled which would include Reckitt & Colman, manufacturers of mustard and other commodities at Norwich and Hull. The Priestmans, the Ellis family and others played a leading part in the woollen milling industries of Bradford, and at Wellington in Somerset, Fox Brothers, renowned to generations of officers in the British and Indian Armies for their puttees, are still well-known for their high grade cloth. C. & J. Clark, shoe manufacturers of Street, Somerset, and Clark Son and Morland, leather manufacturers of Glastonbury, have maintained a very high reputation for several generations. In the heavy industries there were ironmasters like the Lloyds of Warwickshire, or steel manufacturers like the Doncasters of Sheffield. In Ireland the Goodbodys and Walpoles were prominent in the textile industry. In the North generally the Quaker families had great influence in York, Leeds, Bradford, Darlington and Hull. The Pease family who had coal interests in Yorkshire promoted the Stockton and Darlington Railway, which led to their development of the new community at Middlesbrough.

The fact that Friends were not admitted to Oxford and Cambridge until 1871 severely limited the number of them who found distinction in the fields of science or the professions. There were, however, men like Dr Thomas Hodgkin, after whom Hodgkin's Disease was named, and Allen and Hanbury, the manufacturing chemists, who were all Quakers. One professional family certainly deserves mention, that of Alfred Waterhouse (1793–1873) a Liverpool cotton broker. Amongst his eight children there were Alfred, the prominent architect, Theodore, the solicitor, founder of the firm Waterhouse & Company, and Edwin, the accountant, founder of the firm Price Waterhouse & Company.

It is however in the field of banking that the Quaker families have had their greatest influence on industry and commerce in the 19th and 20th centuries, when finance for major projects both in the UK and throughout the world has been the life blood of prosperity. Of the big four clearing banks surviving, Lloyds, of Birmingham originally, was a Quaker family bank which took over others, particularly in the West

Country, like Fox's Bank of Falmouth. In the Barclay Group more than 25 per cent of the family and local banks taken over by merger were founded or developed under Quaker family names. These include Barclay, Backhouse, Bevan, Birkbeck, Buxton, Gibson, Gillett, Lucas, Leatham, Pease, Penrose, Priestman, Seebohm and Tuke.

The Office has derived material and moral strength over nearly 150 years from close association with leading Quaker financiers and industrialists, taking from them something of the integrity and standards of performance on which the reputation and success of Friends' Provident Life Office have been built. The tradition lives on.

Friends are probably best known today for their part in the excellent work done by Oxfam, of which Michael Rowntree was recently chairman, and for the fine record of the Friends' Service Council in bringing help to many communities throughout the world.

Appendix I Part 2

Some Quaker families who have served the board of FPI

The Tuke Family

Samuel Tuke (1784–1857) *'The father of Friends' Provident Institution'*
Signatory of the Guarantee Bond for £500
Chairman of original committee 1831
Director 1832–46
Treasurer 1841
 At annual gatherings at Ackworth School 1829–31 urged formation of Friendly Society until FPI was formed in 1832.
 Tea dealer in York. A city councillor, he did special work for board of health in cholera epidemic in 1832. A founding director of Yorkshire & Fire Life Insurance Company 1824, Savings Bank Movement and Mechanics Friendly Society.
 Recorded Minister of York Meeting and Clerk to London Yearly Meeting 1832–37.

Daniel Tuke (1813–79)
Cousin of Samuel
Director 1845–79
Wholesale Grocer in Bradford

Edward Tuke (1826–91)
Brother of Daniel
Director 1873–91
Wholesale Grocer in Bradford

 Note: Other members of the family were associated with Quaker family banks later merged to form Barclays Bank Ltd, of which Anthony Tuke father and son were chairmen in the 20th century.

The Rowntree Family

Joseph Rowntree (1801–59)
Close associate of Samuel Tuke in formation of FPI
Signatory of the Guarantee Bond for £100
A member of the original committee 1831
Director 1832–59
    At age 21 founded a successful family grocer's business. Keen educationist; on committee of Ackworth School, Bootham School for boys, and The Mount School for girls at York. City councillor in 1858; declined nomination for Lord Mayoralty because 'as chief magistrate he could not conscientiously take or administer an oath'.

John Rowntree (1788–1845)
Elder brother of Joseph
Director 1835–44
    Signatory of the Guarantee Bond for £100. Family grocer at Scarborough. Town councillor and Poor Law guardian at Scarborough. Recorded minister of Scarborough Meeting. In 1818 one of the original committee which founded Bootham School.

John S. Rowntree (1834–1907)
Son of Joseph
Director 1867–1904
Deputy Chairman 1901–02
Grocer and tea merchant in York
    Aged 25 published the influential essay *Quakerism past and present* (1859). Like his father, he was deeply interested in statistics.
    As York city councillor reorganised the finances of the city; Lord Mayor in 1881.

Michael H. Rowntree (1919–   )
Grandson of John S. Rowntree
Director 1956–74
Member of Friends' Ambulance Unit during World War II
Managing Director of Oxford Globe & Mail
Chairman of the Council of Oxfam 1971–77

John Hustler

John Hustler (1768–1841)
First signatory of the Guarantee Bond for £1,000
Member of the original committee 1831
Director and first Treasurer 1832–41
    Farmer, botanist and scholar, prominent and wealthy public figure described as 'the most energetic and progressive man in Bradford'. He founded two schools and provided a market hall in Bradford for the sale of worsted cloth. His presence there influenced the decision to open FPI office at 67/69 Market Street, his property.
    His father, John Hustler (1715–90) designed and operated the important Leeds to Liverpool canal.

The Priestman Family

John Priestman – Bradford (1805–66)
Signatory of Guarantee Bond for £100
Director 1832–66
Chairman 1856–66
Sometime auditor and trustee

Brewing family, later as teetotaller changing to worsted mills in partnership with Seebohm and Ellis families. Reputed for benevolent treatment of millhands, especially women. Introduced profit-sharing scheme.

Keen Free Trader and member of Anti-Corn Law League. Philanthropist and played leading part in Bradford City Council. A minister in Bradford Meeting. He stopped drinking in Quarterly Meeting by turning the tap on during worship to empty the barrel outside.

Samuel Priestman – Kirkstall and Bradford (1800–72)
Brother of John (1805–66)
Father of John (1828–1906)
Signatory of Guarantee Bond for £100
Director 1832–72
Sometime trustee

John Priestman – Bradford (1828–1906)
Son of Samuel and nephew of John (1805–66), father of Henry Brady
Director 1864–1904

Wool spinner and manufacturer in partnership with his brother Alfred. Councillor and alderman of Bradford: chairman of Free Libraries Committee and chairman of Charity Organisation Society.

Frederick Priestman – Bradford (1836–1934)
Director 1867–1915
Chairman 1885–1908
Trustee for most of this period

Member of Finance Committee for 42 years. Resigned from directorship when FPI was incorporated, having no current policy as required by the Rules, but still active in Society of Friends and lived to be 98.

Textile manufacturer. He and his brother built a temperance hall in Bradford in memory of their father. Mayor of Bradford 1882 and 1883.

Henry Brady Priestman – Bradford (1853–1920)
Director 1883–1919
Chairman 1908–17
Trustee for many years

As chairman of FPI visited Canada with Alfred Holmes in 1912: carried through the FPI 1915 Act.

Woollen spinner and manufacturer. Chairman of Chamber of Commerce, City councillor, Chairman of Watch Committee, J.P. Invited to be Mayor of Bradford and candidate for Parliament but refused because he could not, as a teetotaller, entertain appropriately; keen captain of Manningham Cricket Club but resigned when a bar was added to the new pavilion; vigorous in Band of Hope and temperance work. With his brother Walter, promoted adult schools for men and women. Chairman of Bradford Central Liberal Association.

George E. Priestman – Bradford and Ilkley (1863–1942)
Grandson of John (1805–66)
Director 1915–19
   Retired from board when FP&CLO moved to London, and then local director at Bradford.
   Worsted manufacturer

The Seebohm Family

Benjamin Seebohm (1797–1871)
Signatory of Guarantee Bond for £100
Director 1832–71
Founding trustee
Member of Investment & General Committee
   Came from Pyrmont in Germany in 1814 to stay with John Hustler. Related by marriage to the Ellis and Priestman families and was associated with them first in brewing and later in cloth milling in Bradford.
   In 1863 he moved to Luton near his son Frederic at Hitchin.
   Both he and his wife, as appointed Ministers, took active parts in the work of Friends in Yorkshire and Hertfordshire.

Frederic Seebohm (1833–1912)
Son of Benjamin, held brief appointment as a clerk in FPI office at Bradford at a salary of £20/40 per annum – 1852–55, but left to follow a long and successful banking career which led to his becoming a director of Barclays Bank in London.

Hugh E. Seebohm (1867–1945)
Son of Frederic Seebohm (1833–1912)
Director 1922–45
Chairman 1939–44
   Guiding the Office through the very difficult war years he carried through important changes in the Rules in 1942.
   Starting his banking career in his father's firm in Hitchin he became a partner and then a director after amalgamation with Barclays Bank.

Frederic – Lord Seebohm of Hertford (1909–   )
Son of Hugh
Director 1953–79
Chairman 1962–68
   Chairman of Barclays International Ltd. and Deputy Chairman of Barclays Bank Limited. Chairman of a Committee on Local Authority and Allied Personal Social Services. Work in wide field of financial, educational and charitable interests recognised as Knight Bachelor 1970 and Life Peer 1972.

The Barber Family

Christopher Barber,
deputy chairman

James Henry Barber – Sheffield (1820–1902)
Director 1878–1902
    Chairman Sheffield Banking Co. Ltd., Town Trustee, Treasurer Sheffield School Board, JP, Minister of Society of Friends, a founder of Sheffield Friends First Day Schools 1845.

William Bayldon Barber – Sheffield (1874–1939)
Grandson of James Henry
Director 1934–38
    Stockbroker in Sheffield and director of Marcroft Wagon
    Active in developing major games at Bootham and other Friends' schools.

Christopher Bayldon Barber FCA – Reading (1921–)
Director 1970–
Deputy Chairman 1975–
    Finance director, Associated Biscuit Manufacturers Ltd. (Huntley & Palmers Foods). Chairman Social Responsibility Council of the Society of Friends 1970–72 and again, with chairmanship of Education Department, 1979–81.

Note: The following were also closely associated with FPI:

Jarvis W. Barber (1846–1921) ⎤ *Sons of*   ⎤ *Partners of Barber Bros. &*
James H. Barber (1854–1918) ⎬ *James Henry Barber* ⎬ *Wortley – later Jarvis Barber & Sons of Sheffield,*
Harold P. Barber (1872–1929) ⎦ *Son of Jarvis W. Barber* ⎦ *first professional auditors of the Office 1892–1919*

The Clark Family

Bancroft Clark, director

Francis J. Clark – Street (1853–1938)
Son of James Clark (1811–1906) founding partner of C. & J. Clark, shoe manufacturers of Street, Somerset.
Director 1905–33
    Partner and chairman of C. & J. Clark. Local councillor and active supporter of Quaker, temperance and Liberal causes.

W. Bancroft Clark – Street (1902–)
Great-nephew of Francis J. Clark
Director 1934–70
    Chairman C. & J. Clark Ltd 1942-70 carrying through extensive development of the company's business both in UK and overseas, after World War II.

Jan S. Clark – Street (1935–)
Son of W. Bancroft Clark
Director 1971–79
    Director of C. & J. Clark Ltd

168

A Quaker criticism
1872

The following extracts are taken from a long letter published in *The Manchester Friend*, a short-lived rival to *The Friend*, which voiced the views of Friends in Lancashire at a time when the influence of Yorkshire Friends at the head office of FPI was being challenged. A Committee of Conference to advise the directors on nominations for office had been instituted in 1869.

Friends' Provident Institution

To the Editor of the "Manchester Friend."
No. 2.–Nepotism.
11th Month, 4th, 1872.
Dear Friend,

THE statement made at the last Annual Meeting held at Ackworth, as to the strong effort at centralizing the power of this NATIONAL Institution in a Board of Directors, of whom all, *save one*, are Yorkshire men, so closely related to each other that the Board was little better than "a family pie," having been called in question, wilt thou kindly allow space to show some of the data sustaining the remark.

*   *   *   *   *   *

It must not be supposed that this paper is the work of any one individual, *unaided*, for the Members are deeply indebted to *many* of their fellow-assurers, up and down the country, for the information herein contained.

Had it not been for the utter obstinacy of the Directors, in withstanding the just rights and liberties of the Members, at the late Annual Meeting, when nepotism was opposed, and the unparalleled presumption of the Secretary, this exposure would probably not have taken place.

The names and residences of each of the eighteen Directors are here given, together with *some* of the results of the enquiries which have been made as to the relationships existent between them, the Arbitrators, and the Auditors.

Read it; and once only will be sufficient to show, Q. E. D., that nepotism reigns throughout.

Directors.
1. John Wilson, Bradford, was formerly in partnership with George Binns. (See also his (indirect) connection with J. J. Dymond, as a business partner at this very time.)
2. George Binns, Bradford, is brother-in-law to Matthew Ridgway, and was formerly in partnership with John Wilson.
3. Daniel Tuke, Bradford, is own brother to E. Tuke; and father-in-law to F. Priestman.

4. Edward Tuke, Bradford, is brother to D. Tuke; uncle to F. Priestman; and cousin to J. S. Rowntree.

5. John Priestman, Bradford, is son of Joshua Priestman, who has been an Arbitrator for about thirty years; is first cousin to F. Priestman; cousin to J. Edmondson; and brother-in-law to one of D. Tuke's daughters.

6. Frederick Priestman, Bradford, is son-in-law to Daniel Tuke; brother-in-law to J. Edmondson; nephew to E. Tuke; first cousin to J. Priestman; &c.

7. Alfred Jesper, Bradford, is brother-in-law to Edward West.

8. William Henry Crossley, Bradford, is uncle to the new Auditor, Wm. C. Parker, and also to John Stansfield.

9. Edward West, Bradford, is brother-in-law to Alfred Jesper.

10. Joseph Thorp, Halifax, is cousin to Thomas Wilson.

11. Joseph Edmondson, Halifax, is brother-in-law to F. Priestman; cousin to J. Priestman; and is in partnership with Joshua Smithson's brother Joseph.

12. Joshua Smithson, Halifax, has a brother in partnership with J. Edmondson.

13. Thomas Wilson, Thornton-in-Craven, is cousin to Joseph Thorp; and brother-in-law to John Stansfield, the oldest and hardest-working clerk in the office, although he has not been the best paid for many years. T W has never insured in the FPI.

14. John S. Rowntree, York, is cousin to E. Tuke, and to Samuel Priestman, who died last spring, and has a business connection *indirectly* with J. J. Dymond.

15. Henry Fryer, Huddersfield, is brother-in-law to Thomas Harvey.

16. Matthew Ridgway, Dewsbury, is brother-in-law to George Binns.

17. Thomas Satterthwaite, Alderley Edge, is brother-in-law to Joseph Firth.

18. Thomas Harvey, Leeds, is brother-in-law to Henry Fryer.

Of the above eighteen Directors only *one* does not belong to Yorkshire Quarterly Meeting; and of the remainder, *fifteen* belong to Brighouse Monthly Meeting, and of these no fewer than *nine* are Bradford men, to whom must be added Joseph John Dymond, he being, as he signs himself, "the Principal Officer managing the Life Assurance Business."

Arbitrators.
Joshua Priestman, Thornton (who for some years has, through age and infirmities, been incompetent for *any* business) is father of J. Priestman; uncle to F. Priestman; and father-in-law to one of D. Tuke's daughters.

John T. Rice, Bentham (recently elected as Arbitrator,) is Manager of the "Bentham Joint Stock Flax Mills, Limited," of which company Joseph John Dymond is a partner.

Joseph Firth, High Flatts, is brother-in-law to T. Satterthwaite.

John S. Rowntree is, also, a *Director!* (See relations,) and has also a business interest through Joseph Rowntree (of York,) with J. J. Dymond, J. T. Rice, J. Wilson, and others; and, as such, neither J. S. Rowntree nor J. T. Rice is eligible to act as a disinterested party in cases of arbitration.

Auditors.
Up to 1871, the Auditors were also Directors!

William C. Parker, is nephew to W. H. Crossley, and brother-in-law to John Stansfield and Thomas Wilson.

Joseph Edmondson is also a *Director;* and as Auditor, has to examine the accounts prepared by the Directors! Is he eligible to act in either position while he holds the other?

Clerks.
Joseph John Dymond, Bradford, is a partner with John Wilson, Joseph Rowntree (of York,) and others, in the "Bentham Joint Stock Flax Mills, Limited," although receiving at least £1,000 a year as "Secretary and Resident Actuary," with seven clerks to assist him, who draw £779. 12s. 3d. *or less*, between them.

John Stansfield is brother-in-law to T. Wilson, and also to W. C. Parker, the new auditor, and is nephew to W. H. Crossley.

*   *   *   *   *   *

More of these relationships could be given if time and space permitted; but the above are surely sufficient to satisfy anyone asking if the Board, &c., were *really* a "family pie."

*   *   *   *   *   *

Is this state of things to continue?

Thy Friend, sincerely,
An Insurer of Some Years' Standing

Appendix II

The Century Insurance Company Ltd overseas, 1919-74

THIS STORY OF The Century and its subsidiaries in overseas territories concerns its short-term business, mainly fire and motor. Major issues are dealt with in the chapters relating to FP & CLO, but some details elaborate the record for the main areas. The period 1918–74 falls into three phases. First 1918–45 when Henry Tapscott built up the USA and Canadian branches, largely as a source of investment funds and he had to weather the storms of the Depression and World War II. Secondly 1946–57 when Douglas Pringle with the help of Jack Tranter reinforced the USA and Canadian branches, established branches in the place of agencies in Australia and South Africa, expanding to Central Africa, East Africa and Nigeria, and increased the number of agencies in Europe, Middle East and the West Indies. Thirdly 1957–74 when David Tregoning continued to expand The Century's branches in Central Africa and Nigeria and opened a branch in New Zealand, but was forced by circumstances reluctantly to withdraw The Century from USA, and had to close down, on account of nationalism, all the branches in Africa. In this last period Jack Tranter, Robin Gray and Brian Stone directed the overseas department and visited the branches.

Jack Tranter, deputy general manager

Throughout the period of 57 years The Century as a small but well respected company had to contend with many and various underwriting difficulties, but overall the branches were able to maintain viability in all the territories except the USA, and the staff maintained the high standards of the company. The ongoing success however lay in the way in which The Century prepared the path for Friends' Provident's overseas operations, first in Central Africa, then in the purchase of

Fidelity in Canada, and later, in 1960, for the branch of the parent office in Australia which in the late '70s was to enjoy outstanding success.

Larry Tillman, USA manager

USA

The Century had been writing fire business in the USA since 1911 in the office of Henry W. Brown & Company of Philadelphia, who had an office in New York. Under the American general agency system the business, proportionately shared by several insurance companies, was handled under a commission and expenses contract by general agents. They appointed local agents for their companies, underwrote their business, made reinsurance arrangements, issued policies and paid claims. The business in fact belonged to the general agent who was backed by insurers carrying the risk. In addition to the introductory commission, a profit commission, of the order of 10 per cent, could be earned by the general agent on underwriting profits made for the companies. The business of The Century handled in this way was for the most part written in the Eastern and Southern States. It seemed right for a small company to be wary of becoming involved in disasters such as the San Francisco Earthquake or the Chicago Conflagration. The business ran profitably for the company from 1911 to 1918, but in the immediate post-war period competition forced down to uneconomic levels all premium rates, which had to be approved in each State by politically minded State Commissioners. The leading American companies, followed later by the larger British companies, were ready to accept a degree of underwriting loss at a time when they were enjoying large capital profits on their invested trading reserves, but for the small Century operation the strain was becoming intolerable. Henry Tapscott in his report to the board in 1923 commented disapprovingly on this philosophy, and it is amusing to find him reporting to the board 10 years later that heavy underwriting losses could be accepted having regard to the interest and capital profits earned on the funds of both Friends' Provident and The Century accumulated in the USA.

The seriousness of the situation in 1922 can be judged by the fact that The Century's premium income in the USA at £125,000 was approximately 60 per cent of the company's total fire premium income world-wide. The loss ratio in 1920 was 102.7 per cent rising in 1921 to 109 per cent at a time when the overall premium income was increasing at the rate of 30 per cent per annum. When Henry Tapscott freed himself that year to make the first of his visits to the USA and Canada he was able to correct the situation. He encouraged the writing of the lighter dwelling-house and small business risks and also, on the advice of Henry

I. Brown, took a share of a pool arranged by W. Brandt Inc of San Francisco writing all-risks insurance covering personal valuables. This class of risk was traditionally hazardous, but the experience of this pool proved very satisfactory over a number of years. These measures brought the United States account back into profit, and by 1925 the premium income written by Henry W. Brown & Company had been doubled. The subsidiary Pacific Coast Fire of Vancouver started in 1926 to write American business for both The Century and PCF in the three Western states, Washington, Oregon and California, making it possible to improve the status of The Century in the American market by quoting the net assets of the Century Group, available in the USA, at the impressive figure of over one million dollars. The renewed profitability of the underwriting account led Henry Tapscott to exploit his very keen interest in the investment field during the mid '20s at a time when the American financial world was on the crest of a wave of optimism, with no hint of the disaster which the Depression was to bring them in 1929.

In 1927 there were discrepancies in the accounting system in Henry Brown's Office but no serious defalcation was revealed. Walter Stone and Larry Tillman, both of whom were later to become managers of The Century USA branch, were commended for their part in correcting the situation, but in 1928 Bernard Brigham, head office accountant of Friends' Provident, had to pay a long visit to New York to sort out, amongst other things, an unexplained loss of $180,000. At the end of 1928 Henry I. Brown found himself compelled, by the action of the bank, to find a purchaser for his controlling interest in the Liberty Bell Insurance Company and, as The Century, his leading company, were not prepared to take it over, he sold it to a group of New York fire insurance companies, giving them a dominating interest in the insurance side of Henry W. Brown & Company. This did not suit The Century and after terminating the general agency agreement a Century USA branch was set up in New York. Walter Stone of Henry W. Brown & Company was appointed joint manager for the USA with Bill McConnell, the very able manager of the Dublin office of FP & CLO.

The Century wrote after 1920 a growing USA marine account managed by the Commercial Union in New York and by general agents Rathbone King and Seeley in San Francisco, who reported direct to the London underwriter – first Arthur Davies, and later Frank Hotine and Philip Freeborn. Over a period of 40 years the surplus was generally satisfactory, but there were times when results fluctuated violently.

The New York branch under Bill McConnell began life in the worst possible circumstances as the crisis of 1929–32 plunged the United States into the agony of the great Depression. The new manager's instructions, before he even got the branch operation working fully, were to trim back his underwriting and to cut staff and all expenses to a minimum; worse still, a 10 per cent cut in salaries, was to follow in 1931. Very heavy underwriting losses were incurred in both fire and accident departments and relations between the new branch manager and the general agents were severely strained. The situation was further aggravated by the disruptive operation of converting The Century in the USA from non-tariff to tariff. Through the ensuing years of the Depression the establishment of the USA branch was a gruelling task. Only in the marine department was any underwriting profit earned before the turn of the tide in 1934, and it took longer still for the investment market to recover. The disproportionate and unprofitable growth of the company's fire business in the USA, was becoming intolerable. Motor business too, attractive to general agents for its volume, showed a worsening trend of underwriting losses. In 1936 Henry Tapscott approached first the Commercial Union, The Century's marine managers, and secondly the Norwich Union, seeking a management or pooling arrangement, but without success. It was decided therefore, without fully appreciating the extent to which the general agents themselves would be losing their hold on the American market, that the branch must continue its general agency operation.

These investigations brought to a head the question of replacing Bill McConnell as manager of the USA branch. He had achieved much in setting up the branch, but, at age 65 and suffering from acute arthritis, he could not manage the extensive travelling called for and he was allowed to retire in March 1938. In his place the directors appointed Larry Tillman who had been first with Henry W. Brown & Company and since 1930 with The Century branch on the accounts and investment side for 12 years. A branch secretary, Roland Gwyn, was sent out from London, with a view to his succeeding in due course, but his promotion was delayed until 1948 because he volunteered to serve throughout the War with the Royal Canadian Air Force. He succeeded Larry Tillman as US manager in 1953, holding the appointment until the branch was closed in 1963. That period of 10 years saw a constant battle against underwriting losses and rising costs and Roland Gwyn did well to hold selected business from the declining body of general agents and to keep the loyalty of his staff in New York. For nearly 20 years after the closing of the branch he kept in touch with all the Century pensioners with a six-monthly 'Newsletter'.

Canada

The initiative of Henry Brown, general manager of The Century in Edinburgh, led to the acceptance in 1908 of the offer from the Pacific

Pacific Coast Fire's first office, Cordova Street, Vancouver, BC, 1890

Coast Fire Insurance Company of Vancouver BC to manage a fire account for The Century in Western Canada in return for reinsurance in Edinburgh of the PCF's guarantee business. In 1920 the PCF was taken over and that company then managed all underwriting in Canada for The Century and its subsidiaries. General agencies were established in Toronto, Winnipeg and Montreal, and by 1931 when the company was writing fire business on a Dominion-wide licence further agents were appointed in Regina, Halifax and St Johns'. Concentrating on the lighter risk areas of the West and Maritime States the underwriting experience was good, and until the Depression came to Canada, rather later than it did in the USA, investment conditions were equally satisfactory. In 1930 Canada changed from the non-tariff to the tariff section of the fire and accident markets, conforming with the practice of The Century in the UK and USA.

It was inevitable that Canada, with a population of only 10 million, would feel the blast of the economic blizzard which had swept across the continent in 1929, but there were factors in Canada which lessened its effect north of the border. The Canadian economy was supported by a sound banking system on a Dominion-wide foundation, and in the insurance industry, the Canadian Underwriters' Association, which controlled the tariff companies on a Dominion basis, was a far more reliable organisation than its counterpart in the USA. There was as yet no branch organisation in Canada, but the PCF had well established general agents in the major cities of all the provinces. Under the rules of the Canadian Underwriters' Association a member company was not

Thomas Greer, managing director Pacific Coast Fire

Policy Register	PACIFIC COAST FIRE INSURANCE COMPANY						Page one
Policy No	Name and Residence	Commencement	Expiration	Amount	Rate	Premium	Copy of Policy
1	Charles Hay Esq Vancouver, B.C.	27 August, 1890	27 August, 1893.	1500	140	21 00	(a) £1250. On his one and one-half storey frame, shingle-roofed dwelling including porches.

Additions and ornamental work thereto. Situate on lots 3 and 4, the South side of Alexander Street, City of Vancouver, B.C.
(B) £250. On his grand square piano while contained in the above described dwelling. Special reference being had to the Assured's application No. 1, which is his Warranty and a part hereof.

Pacific Coast Fire, Policy No 1, 27th August 1890

allowed to appoint more than one general agent in each city and in order to get round this rule, as other groups did, The Century had introduced two UK subsidiaries, the Anglo-Scottish and the Southern. As chief executives of the largest, albeit small, general insurance company in Western Canada, Thomas Greer, followed by Bob Nightingale, were members of the Dominion board of the Canadian Underwriters' Association, which brought added status to the PCF, and later to The Century. A satisfactory record of fire profits was maintained up to and through World War II, but predictably steps had to be taken to cut back on the motor account which was running into underwriting losses by 1937 and 1938.

Since a visit to Canada by the chairman, Henry B. Priestman and Alfred Holmes in 1912, Friends' Provident had maintained a mortgage portfolio managed by William Gregory in Toronto, and by Black and Armstrong in Winnipeg. In 1936 Vernon Armstrong took over from William Gregory, and he maintained this close connection with the Office for over 40 years. When additional trading reserves were needed The Century Insurance Trust subscribed a further $500,000 for new ordinary shares of the Pacific Coast Fire. The economy of Canada emerged from the Depression rather more rapidly than that of the USA and by 1939 The Century's underwriting account and investment portfolio were both firmly based to face the strain of the next six years of war. Bob Nightingale was sent out to succeed Thomas Greer in 1942 as managing director of PCF and manager for Canada of The Century. Harry Cutler took over from him in 1953.

Australia

The earliest record of The Century operating in Australia is the appointment in 1911 of J. Hassall & Company of Sydney as managing agents for New South Wales to write fire, accident and employers' liability business. In the next year agents were appointed in Victoria and Queensland reporting through this general agency. In 1914, however, after very heavy claims experience Hassall's agency was dissolved and new agents, M. De Chateaubourg and Matthews, were appointed with additional authority for writing marine business. They also had, for a brief period in 1915, authority to accept reassurance of life business from the National Mutual Life Association of Australasia for policies not exceeding £1,500 on any one life. This agency agreement continued until 1927 when an Australian branch office was opened at Sydney with John Waddell as manager and M. De Chateaubourg under him as marine manager. State managers were appointed for New South Wales, Victoria and South Australia with a managing agent in Queensland. Things, however, did not go well for the branch, and the directors considered pulling out of Australia altogether until Harry Daniel, fire manager in London, visited Sydney in 1928 and advised against this course.

After approaches to several British companies an agreement was signed with the Northern to be managers of The Century from their office in Melbourne. The fire experience was reasonably profitable, but in the accident account heavy losses were sustained. The Northern gave notice to terminate in 1938 and an agreement was signed in 1939 with the Royal Exchange which continued satisfactorily throughout the war. It was not until 1950 that a new arrangement was made.

Craig Grainger, manager for Belfast, was sent out to Sydney in 1949 to set up a new Century branch. In January 1951 this came into being with State managers at Sydney and Melbourne, and chief agents at Brisbane, Adelaide and Perth. Subsequently Brisbane and Adelaide became branches and a chief agent was appointed at Hobart, where there was a strong Quaker community. The standing of The Century in the Australian market was enhanced by taking on the management for Australia of other European insurers, the Copenhagen Re, the Hibernian of Dublin, and the Fylgia of Stockholm. Throughout the 25 years during which The Century branch was a member of the Group in Australia, the fire profits were fairly consistent but the accident results fluctuated violently, especially in the motor and liability departments. A strong Australian board of directors, introduced in the early days by Craig Grainger included Major-General Sir Denzil Macarthur-Onslow, CBE, DSO, ED, a direct descendant of John Macarthur the famous 18th-century pioneer of New South Wales, and also Lawford Richardson and John Westgarth. In 1957 General Sir John Northcott, KCMG, KCVO, CB,

Robin Gray, assistant general manager

was appointed chairman after he retired from his appointment as Governor of New South Wales. They all did much to enhance the prestige of The Century in Australia and to prepare the ground on which Friends' Provident was able to enter the field in 1960 with a life branch.

South Africa

The Century after World War I developed new branch connections in many parts of the African Continent. The first venture was the setting up of a branch in 1922 in Cape Town with Colonel Sir John Hewat as manager for Cape Province, later manager for South Africa. This arrangement, however, lasted for only two years and The Century's account was then put into the hands of the Louis Siff general agency at Johannesburg covering the Union of South Africa, Rhodesia and South West Africa. Over the next five years its territory was extended to include Kenya, Uganda, Tanganyika, Nyasaland and Portuguese East Africa. The volume of premium income written grew steadily but the underwriting results were very erratic so, after financial difficulties in 1928, Douglas Fordham was seconded from head office to establish a branch office at Johannesburg jointly with Louis Siff whose resignation was accepted a year later. Douglas Fordham remained as manager until 1932 when, in the atmosphere of the Depression, the branch was closed and an agreement was signed with the Phoenix Assurance Company for management in all these territories. This happy relationship with the Phoenix was to last for 21 years and preserved The Century's name in Africa during World War II.

In 1949 George Gordon was appointed resident inspector in Cape Town and he opened a branch there in 1953, after the termination of the Phoenix agreement. Central Africa was detached as a branch at Salisbury, Rhodesia, and the three East African colonies were managed by a new branch at Nairobi, in Kenya. The Century managed the Hibernian of Dublin in South Africa and Rhodesia from 1955 to 1963 when the Hibernian was taken over by the Commercial Union.

After the withdrawal of South Africa from the Commonwealth in 1961, the changes in the political climate gradually forced many British insurance companies to domesticate or close their branch operations. The Century branch, which had been moved from Cape Town to Johannesburg in 1957, was too small for conversion into a local company so, after an unsuccessful search for a possible merger, an offer was accepted in 1969 from the AA Mutual Insurance Association of Johannesburg to take over The Century's business in the Union in return for an equity interest in that company and a share in their reinsurance treaty.

Central Africa

At the time when the branch in Salisbury was detached from South Africa in 1953 under Ken Fenn its territory covered the Federation of Rhodesia which comprised Northern and Southern Rhodesia and Nyasaland; a separate branch at Nairobi controlled Kenya, Uganda and Tanzania. The general business, mainly in the fire department, showed a good record of profit. Progress was greatly assisted by the investment of Friends' Provident funds at attractive rates in industrial loans, and also by the formation in Rhodesia in 1957 of the Rhodesian Century Building Society, managed by Douglas Macpherson.

In 1954, encouraged by the success of The Century, a start was made in writing life and pensions business in the Federation in Rhodesian currency. The management and underwriting of the account were kept in London, with Salisbury office of The Century being used as a shop window. It was considered, quite rightly, that this form of remote control would not be acceptable for South Africa and John Robson was not prepared to face the political risk of setting up a fully independent branch in the Union to cover both South Africa and Rhodesia. With good support from The Century a Friends' Provident life account with a large element of pension business was written in the local currency. In 1957 the life account was extended to East Africa based on The Century branch at Nairobi, where the prevailing political unrest led to a demand for policies to be issued in sterling as well as in the local currency. A separate life series had to be written after 1964 in Zambia when it was declared an independent state.

Brian Stone, assistant general manager and general manager of The Century in the Phoenix Group

In 1964 Hudson Adams from Nairobi succeeded Ken Fenn at Salisbury and James Jeffery took over the branch in independent Zambia at Lusaka. In 1970 general insurance in Zambia was nationalised and Friends' Provident stopped writing life business also.

In 1965 the Unilateral Declaration of Independence in Rhodesia brought to an end the life underwriting in the colony and a large sum representing the surplus of assets over liabilities was frozen until after the state of Zimbabwe was granted independence in 1980.

In Kenya and Uganda the life account was closed in 1964 and the Tanzanian life insurance industry was nationalised in 1967. New legislation compelled the withdrawal of The Century from all the East African territories, and the Zambian branch at Lusaka was closed. During the years of UDI in Rhodesia, Hudson Adams managed the Friends' Provident life and investment interests and developed the very profitable general account written in the name of a Rhodesian Century company taken over by the Phoenix in 1975. He subsequently became managing director of the leading Zimbabwean company.

Nigeria

During the '50s and '60s the Office developed satisfactory life and general accounts in Nigeria, a proportion of the life business being written for students and others temporarily resident in the UK. Here again by acquiring the Lagos Building Society, and forming The Century Mortgage Company, loan facilities assisted development, but compulsory domestication brought this to an end in 1968. The two resulting companies were sold to the Commercial Union.

So ended the Office's ventures in Africa where for over 20 formative years FP & CLO had shared with the leading British offices in the establishment of much needed life and general insurance services in some of the developing nations of the old Commonwealth, a disappointing end to a worthwhile and profitable effort.

New Zealand

The last branch operation overseas opened in 1957 by The Century was in New Zealand at Auckland under the managership of Leslie Westlake, who had been manager in Nairobi for seven years. Within a year, however, he resigned and was succeeded by Cyril Sead-Gowing, a New Zealander who, with his father, had for many years managed the account in New Zealand of the Excess Insurance Company of London. He firmly established The Century in the strongly traditional New Zealand insurance market, with the support of a local board under the chairmanship of Ian Reid of Wellington. When he retired in 1964 he handed over to Angus Sharpe and the office was moved to Wellington, where a strong and profitable account, based on brokers (who were not universally well regarded by local competitors) was built up over the 10 years before The Century was taken over by the Phoenix. Thoughts of starting a New Zealand life fund were rejected on the ground that the competition was already very keen in a country with a limited scope for expansion in its economy.

Denmark

Amongst the other overseas operations of The Century which should be mentioned, the most interesting was the purchase in 1953, through the close relationship enjoyed with the Copenhagen Re of the small Danish insurance company the Urania of Copenhagen. For a period of 13 years under the management of Erik Gamst this company wrote a small but profitable account in Denmark, with reinsurance arrangements in other

Scandinavian countries, until once again in 1966 changes in local legislation influenced the decision to take a profit when the original vendors showed themselves ready to re-purchase the company.

Other Overseas Territories

In the days when the policy of spreading risks led even the biggest groups to keep their retentions to percentages which today seem very small, there was ample room for a well respected office like The Century to take a share of the business offered by general agencies in many parts of the world.

In India, with Pakistan after 1948, the Caledonian Insurance Company of Edinburgh was appointed manager in 1932 and wrote for The Century an almost consistently profitable account, mainly in the fire department, for over 40 years; this management agreement continued even after the absorption of the Caledonian into the Guardian Group in 1957.

Strong agencies were established for Europe, in Belgium, France, Germany, Greece, Holland and Portugal and, for the Middle East, in Egypt and Cyprus. Further afield agencies were opened in the East at Shanghai, Hong Kong, Saigon, Bangkok, Penang, Rangoon and Manila, and for the West Indies in Jamaica, Trinidad and Barbados.

On the whole these foreign agencies contributed over the years a welcome addition to the profits of the fire department and, to a lesser extent, to those of the accident department with full control of the commission and expenses involved in their administration. A further volume of profitable overseas business came from participating with other companies and Lloyd's on the schedules of foreign business written in London.

Another important function of the overseas department was the handling of negotiations for inwards and outwards reinsurance treaties for the short-term business. In this connection particularly friendly relations were enjoyed with the Swiss Re Copenhagen Re and Munich Re as well as the leading offices and brokers in the London market. Jack Tranter and his successors Robin Gray and Brian Stone made a number of tours overseas performing a very useful role keeping in touch with directors, staff and agents on their own ground, and providing hospitality for those who visited London and Dorking. This was particularly helpful when Friends' Provident was using The Century branch organisation and connections in opening life operations in Africa and Australia and absorbing Fidelity Life in Canada.

Appendix III

Directors and executives of the Office
1832~1981

CHAIRMEN

Friends' Provident Institution 1832–1919

Samuel Tuke	pro tem	1834	John Snowden	1849–1851
Samuel Gurney	pro tem	1835	David Smith	1852
John Snowden	pro tem	1836	John Snowden	1853–1855
James Ellis	pro tem	1837–1838	John Priestman	1856–1866
John Wilson	pro tem	1839	John Wilson	1867–1873
Samuel Gurney	pro tem	1840	Edward West	1873–1883
William West	pro tem	1841	John Wilson	1884–1885
John Wilson	pro tem	1842	Frederick Priestman	1885–1908
James Ellis	pro tem	1843	Henry B. Priestman	1908–1917
John Wilson	pro tem	1844–1846	Alfred Holmes	1917–1919*
James Ellis		1847–1848		*See FP & CLO

Friends' Provident & Century Life Office 1920–1973

Alfred Holmes	1920–1927	Lord Franks	1955–1962
Harold Morland	1928–1939	Lord Seebohm	1962–1968
Hugh Seebohm	1939–1945	Edwin Phillips	1968–1973*
Herbert Tanner	1945–1955		*See FPLO

Friends' Provident Life Office 1973–

Edwin Phillips	1973–

182

DIRECTORS

Friends' Provident Institution 1832–1919

Benjamin Seebohm	1832–1871	Thomas Harvey	1849–1873
Samuel Gurney	1832–1855	John Wilson	1849–1892
John Hustler	1832–1841	Edward West	1850–1883
James Foster	1832–1837	Sir Robert Fowler	1852–1858
Newman Cash	1832–1866	Alfred Harris, Junr	1852–1858
John Hipsley	1832–1859	Joseph Barclay	1856–1871
Robert Arthington	1832–1836	Henry Gurney	1856–1867
Samuel Priestman	1832–1872	Thomas Satterthwaite	1858–1873
John Armistead	1832–1844	Joseph Edmondson	1861–1881
George Crosfield	1832–1847	Henry Fryer	1861–1882
Joseph Rowntree	1832–1859	John Priestman, Junr	1864–1904
William West	1832–1852	Joseph Pease	1867–1871
James Ellis	1832–1870	Frederick Priestman	1867–1915
John Priestman	1832–1866	John S. Rowntree	1867–1903
Samuel Tuke	1832–1857	Joshua Smithson	1868–1903
William Hoyland	1832–1835		
David Smith	1832–1853	Edward Tuke	1873–1891
Thomas Fowler	1832–1851	Alfred Jesper	1873–1904
Joseph Pim	1832–1840	Matthew Ridgway	1873–1879
John Snowden	1832–1855	Joseph Beck	1874–1891
Thomas Walker	1832–1848	John Edmondson	1874–1885
Alfred Harris, Senr	1835–1839	Henry Fowler	1874–1879
Joseph Thorp	1835–1873	Theodore Fry	1874–1877
Thomas Wilson	1835–1873	John Thorp	1874–1893
Henry Pearson	1835–1871	George Baker	1875–1908
Henry Crossley	1835–1899	James Barber	1878–1902
William Alexander	1835–1840		
John Rowntree	1835–1844	Robert Parkinson	1882–1906
Thomas Backhouse	1835–1844	James Richardson	1883–1890
John Wilson	1837–1838	Henry B. Priestman	1884–1919
John Wilson, Junr	1837–1846	Thomas Emmott	1886–1892
Josiah Forster	1838–1870		
George Binns	1839–1879	Henry Tuke Mennell	1891–1913
Robert Crossland	1839–1855	Richard Clark	1892–1916
John Thistlethwaite	1839–1862	William Wells	1893–1914
		Charles Binns	1893–1912
Robert Jowitt	1845–1860		
Joseph Holmes	1846–1854	William Harvey	1900–1913
Daniel Tuke	1846–1879	Alfred Holmes	1904–1919*
Henry Crosfield	1848–1872	Alfred Simpson	1904–1915

See FP & CLO

Francis Clark	1905–1919*	George Priestman	1915–1919*
John Whiting	1905–1920	Harold Morland	1915–1919*
Robert Marsh	1906–1919*	David Dreghorn Binnie	1919–1919*
Harrison Barrow	1907–1919*	Henry Brown	1919–1919*
H. Borrough Hopkins	1908–1919*		
Thomas Hodgkin	1915–1919*		*See FP & CLO*

Friends' Provident & Century Life Office 1920–1973

Alfred Holmes	1920–1928	Kenneth Wilson	1947–1958
Francis Clark	1920–1933	William Brown	1948–1952
Robert Marsh	1920–1941	Philip Priestman	1949–1963
Harrison Barrow	1920–1946	Sir Douglas Marshall	1950–1973*
H. Borrough Hopkins	1920–1933	Lord Franks	1953–1962
Thomas Hodgkin	1920–1921	Lord Rowallan	1953–1959
Harold Morland	1920–1939		1963–1966
David Dreghorn Binnie	1920–1936	Lord Seebohm	1953–1973*
Henry Brown	1920–1922	Julian Fox	1954–1967
Sir John Halliday Croom	1922–1923	Leonard Gray	1956–1964
Hugh Crosfield	1922–1944	Michael Rowntree	1956–1973*
Hugh Seebohm	1922–1945	Michael Cadbury	1956–1973*
Sir John Ewing	1924–1932	Harold Douglas	1959–1973*
Reginald Mounsey	1929–1954	Lord Ferrier	1959–1970
Horace Walpole	1933–1951	Sir Ronald Thornton	1961–1971
John Johnstone	1933–1961	Edwin Phillips	1962–1973*
Bayldon Barber	1934–1938	Ian Johnstone	1964–1973*
Bancroft Clark	1934–1970	Paul Tapscott	1966–1973*
Alfred Moorhouse	1936–1948	Michael Fox	1967–1973*
Arthur Gray Pickard	1939–1953	David Tregoning	1968–1973*
Herbert Tanner	1940–1958	Sir Charles Carter	1968–1973*
Alfred Braithwaite*	1941–1973	Sir Anthony Touche Bt	1969–1973*
Douglas Foulis	1943–1954	Christopher Barber	1970–1973*
Sir Thomas Holland	1943–1946	Archibald Gilchrist	1970–1973*
John Little	1943–1946	Jan Clark	1971–1973*
Robert Wotherspoon	1943–1967	Lord Taylor of Gryfe	1972–1973*
Brian Manning	1945–1962	Bryan Skinner	1972–1973
Henry Tapscott	1945–1950		
Thomas Barlow	1947–1970		*See FPLO*

Friends' Provident Life Office 1973

Alfred Braithwaite	1973–1975	Christopher Barber	1973–
Sir Douglas Marshall	1973–1976	Jan Clark	1973–1979
Lord Seebohm	1973–1979	Archibald Gilchrist	1973–1974
Michael Rowntree	1973–1974	Lord Taylor of Gryfe	1973–
Michael Cadbury	1973–1974	Bill Stubbs	1973–1981
Harold Douglas	1973–	Fred Cotton	1975–
Edwin Phillips	1973–	Lawford Richardson	1977–1981
Ian Johnstone	1973–	Paul Honigmann	1979–1981
Paul Tapscott	1973–	Mike Doerr	1980–
Michael Fox	1973–	Michael Hardie	1980–
David Tregoning	1973–1979	Doug King	1980–
Sir Charles Carter	1973–	Peter Watson	1981–
Sir Anthony Touche Bt	1973–		

EXECUTIVE OFFICERS

Friends' Provident Institution 1832–1919

Secretaries		Consultant Actuaries	
Benjamin Ecroyd	1832–1857	William Newman – Yorkshire	1832–1838
Joseph Dymond	1857–1885	Charles Ansell – Atlas	1838–1873
John Tennant	1886–1904	William Tyndall – Atlas	1873–1877
William Gregory	1904–1916		

		Actuaries	
		Joseph Dymond	1877–1889
		John Tennant	1889–1904
		Alfred Moorhouse	1904–1919

General Manager and Secretary

Henry Tapscott	1916–1919*	*see FP & CLO

Friends' Provident & Century Life Office 1920–1973

General Managers		Actuaries	
Henry Tapscott	1920–1945	Alfred Moorhouse	1920–1936
Douglas Pringle	1945–1957	John Robson	1936–1955
David Tregoning	1957–1973	Dennis Jackson	1956–1971
		Doug King	1971–1973*

Deputy General Managers

Bill Palmer	1955–1959	Dewi Lloyd Humphreys	1969–1970
Jack Tranter	1955–1961	Dennis Jackson	1971–1972
George Palmer	1959–1964	Bill Stubbs	1972–1973*

Chief Assistant General Managers

Harold Cope	1961–1964
Bill Stubbs	1970–1972
Fred Cotton	1972–1973*

Assistant General Managers

Harold Sutcliffe	1928–1943	Robin Gray	1961–1964
Bernard Brigham	1933–1936	Brian Stone	1964–1973*
Charles Bosanquet	1934–1939	Reginald Harding	1965–1970
Harry Daniel	1943–1954	Bill Bailey	1965–1973*
Herbert Rowntree	1946–1948	Michael Brigham	1965–1973*

Secretaries

James Heighton	1920–1924	Samuel Mills	1952–1960
Alfred Moorhouse	1924–1936	Michael Brigham	1960–1965
Bernard Brigham	1936–1952	Raymond Johnson	1965–1973*

*See FPLO

Sam Mills, secretary

Bill Bailey, assistant general manager

Raymond Johnson, secretary

Friends' Provident Life Office 1973–

Chief General Managers

Bill Stubbs	1980–1981
Fred Cotton	1981–

General Managers

Bill Stubbs	1973–1980	Michael Hardie – Investments	1980–
Doug King – Actuary	1980–	Mike Doerr – Operations	1980–

Deputy General Manager

Fred Cotton	1973–1980

Chief Assistant General Manager and Actuary

Doug King	1973–1980

Assistant General Managers

Brian Stone	1973–1974	Colin McWilliam – Personnel	1980–
Bill Bailey	1973–1976	Malcolm Payne – Marketing	1980–
Michael Brigham	1973–1975	Peter Silvester – Pensions	1980–
		Rod Wild – Systems	1980–

Secretaries

Raymond Johnson	1973–1979
Richard Shuker	1979–

Colin McWilliam, assistant general manager, personnel

Malcolm Payne, assistant general manager, marketing

Peter Silvester, assistant general manager, pensions

Richard Shuker, secretary

Chief Medical Officers

LONDON		DORKING	
Dr T. D. Lister	1919–1923	Dr L. J. Barford	1958–1969
Dr T. Thomson	1923–1935	Dr J. R. Partridge	1958–
Dr T. Jenner Hoskin	1924–1954	Dr G. H. Robb	1980–
Dr F. S. Bach	1935–1975	EDINBURGH	
Dr C. Hardwick	1956–1981	Dr J. Playfair	1920–1933
Dr R. D. C. Brackenridge	1959–	Dr W. A. Alexander	1933–1963
Dr K. H. G. Milne	1970–1973	Dr R. F. Robertson	1963–1976
Dr P. H. Kidner	1974–	Dr L. J. P. Duncan	1968–1976

Dr T. Thomson

Dr W. A. Alexander

Dr F. S. Bach

Dr R. D. C. Brackenridge

Dr J. R. Partridge

188

Appendix IV

Statistics

Table 1

Progress over the first 148 years

Figures shown, other than those for 1918 and 1980, are for Bonus Declaration years. Prior to 1902 bonuses declared were at rates varying according to the class of business and the term for which the policy had been in force. Last available figures are for 1980.

Year	Funds £000	Premium Income £000	New Sums Assured £000	Reversionary Bonus £%	Interim Bonus £%	Terminal Bonus %
			FRIENDS' PROVIDENT INSTITUTION			
1842	151	22				
1847	258	31				
1852	389	42				
1857	523	44				
1862	670	53				
1867	831	63				
1872	1,111	90	194			
1877	1,358	102	193			
1882	1,623	111	227			
1887	1,870	148	188			
1892	2,246	185	269			
1897	2,646	191	244			
1902	3,033	203	197	1.10.0	—	
1907	3,368	201	187	1.10.0	1. 0.0	
1912	3,426	191	278	1.12.0	1. 5.0	
1918	3,294	246	784	No declaration before 1919		

Table 1 continued

Year	Funds £000	Premium Income £000	New Sums Assured £000	Reversionary Bonus £%	Interim Bonus £%	Terminal Bonus %
			FRIENDS' PROVIDENT & CENTURY LIFE OFFICE			
1919	3,451	310	1,504	1.10.0	1. 5.0	
1924	4,619	554	1,384	1.16.0	1.16.0	
1929	6,185	688	1,646	2. 2.0	2. 2.0	
1934	9,190	1,480	2,435	1.15.0	1.15.0	
1939	14,391	1,341	2,010)	†		
1944	16,671	1,178	2,110)			
1949	21,640	2,680	9,630	1.10.0	1. 5.0	
1954	39,953	6,422	22,010	2.10.0	2. 5.0	
1959	76,508	11,607	46,020	2.12.6	2.10.0	
1964	147,772	23,185	113,697	3. 0.0 *+15%	2.15.0	
1967	200,000	24,915	155,915	3. 6.0 *+10%	3. 2.0	
1970	261,668	28,476	218,000	4. 0.0	3.16.0	20
1973	357,336	46,908	439,000	4. 0.0	3.16.0	25
			FRIENDS' PROVIDENT LIFE OFFICE			
1976	506,143	67,744‡	758,000	4.40	4.40	20
1979	750,247	108,705‡	1,060,000	4.75	4.75	30
1980	851,520	127,346‡	1,192,000	—	4.75	40

†Notes

War-time declarations:

	Reversionary Bonus		Interim Bonus	
1939		NIL	For 1935/39	£1. 0. 0%
			From 1940	15. 0%
1944	For 1935/39	£1. 0. 0%		
	For 1940/42	NIL		
	For 1943/44	£1. 5. 0%	From 1945	£1. 0. 0%

*Special reversionary bonus calculated on bonuses attached at preceding distribution

‡Including PHI premium income after 1st January 1975

Table 2

Analysis of Investments Held and Yield – 1919–1980

Investments Held

Valuation Year	British Government & Other Fixed Interest %	Mortgages & Loans %	Ordinary Shares %	Property %	Cash %	Total £m	Gross Yield on the Fund £%
FRIENDS' PROVIDENT & CENTURY LIFE OFFICE							
1919	48	47	—	4	1	3	5. 7.11
1924	42	52	—	5	1	4	7. 6. 8**
1929	35	55	2	7	1	6	5.19. 9
1934	59	27	7	6	1	10	5.15. 0
1939	57	24	10	8	1	15	4.16. 0
1944	66	15	11	7	1	17	5. 5. 6
1949	55	25	14	5	1	21	5. 8. 0
1954	32	42†	16	9	1	40	6. 5. 6
1959	29	43	18	9	1	69	6. 2. 5
1964	31	40	22	6	1	148	6. 8. 6
1967	33	38	22	6	1	193	6.18. 8
1970*	24	31	32	11	2	281	7. 8. 5
FRIENDS' PROVIDENT LIFE OFFICE							
1973	30	22	28	19	1	400	7.64
1976‡	46	13	24	16	1	503	10.18
1979	46	7	26	20	1	894	11.47
1980	43	7	30	19	1	1,096	11.70

**Special dividend from The Century

†As from 1954 certain unquoted debentures were reclassified as mortgages

*Market value adopted, apart from mortgages

‡Mortgages valued for first time

Table 3

THE CENTURY INSURANCE COMPANY LIMITED
General Insurance Premium Income 1918–1974

The Century was taken over by Friends' Provident Institution in February 1918

Year	PHI £ooo	Fire £ooo	Accident £ooo	Motor £ooo	Marine £ooo	Total £ooo
1918	26	132	54	—	136	348
1924	26	261	147	—	85	519
1934	37	311	131	109	44	632
1944	45	726	257	94	521	1643
1954	117	2613	735	989	1078	5532
1964	460	3201	1972	2275	1053	8961
1974	1576	28653			4653	34882

The Century was sold to the Phoenix Assurance Company Limited on 31st December 1974

Index

END PAPER

A modern policy as issued by the computer
in 1982

Friends' Provident Life Office

Established 1832 Incorporated by Act of Parliament in the
United Kingdom with limited liability. Registered No. Z115.

POLICY NUMBER	8231937 TABLE 79.K
TYPE OF CONTRACT	Friends' Maxidowment
GRANTEE	David BEVILL

PRINCIPAL OFFICE

PIXHAM END, DORKING, SURREY, RH4 1QA

at which Notices of Assignment may be given in pursuance of the Policies of Assurance Act, 1867.

WHEREAS the person(s) named in the Schedule within as the Grantee(s), being desirous of effecting with the Friends' Provident Life Office (herein called the Office) the Assurance described in the said Schedule on the life (lives) of the person(s) therein named as the Life (Lives) Assured, has (have) delivered to the Office the Proposal(s) mentioned in the said Schedule as the basis of the Contract of Assurance herein contained, it is hereby declared that:

1.   In consideration of the payment to the Office of the first premium and of subsequent premiums (if any) to be paid as provided in the said Schedule, the Office will pay the Sum Assured mentioned in the said Schedule to the person(s) to whom the same is therein expressed to be payable upon proof satisfactory to the Office of

(a) the happening of the event set forth in the said Schedule,

(b) the title of the person(s) claiming payment and

(c) the age(s) of the Life (Lives) Assured or age(s) of the Counter Life (Lives) (if any), if not previously admitted.

2.   This policy is not in force until the First (or Single) Premium has been paid to the Office or, if premiums are expressed in the said Schedule to be payable by monthly payments or by payments at four-weekly intervals, until the first such payment has been paid.

3.   This policy shall be read and construed in accordance with the Governing Law stated in the said Schedule. All monies payable to or by the Office shall be payable at the Paying Office stated in the said Schedule in the currency of the country in which the Paying Office is situated. The payment or acceptance of payment by the Office at any other place will not be deemed to waive this condition as regards any subsequent payments.

4.   This policy shall not be assignable by a minor and the Office shall be under no obligation to take notice of any purported assignment by a minor.

5.   This policy is subject to the conditions specified in the said Schedule and is issued under and subject to the Laws and Rules of the Office.

SIGNED for and on behalf of the Office

F. G. Cotton (signature)

F.G. COTTON

Chief General Manager

Date as Date Risk Assumed in the Schedule within

Examined